Sometimes I Get All Scribbly

Sometimes I Get All Scribbly

Living with Attention-Deficit/ Hyperactivity Disorder

(Revised Edition)

Maureen Bissen Neuville

pro·ed

8700 Shoal Creek Boulevard
Austin, Texas 78757

pro·ed

© 1995, 1991 by PRO-ED, Inc.
8700 Shoal Creek Boulevard
Austin, Texas 78757-6897

Library of Congress Cataloging-in-Publication Data

Neuville, Maureen Bissen.
    Sometimes I Get All Scribbly : Living with Attention Deficit/Hyperactivity Disorder / Maureen Bissen Neuville.—2nd ed.
      p.   cm.
    Includes bibliographical references and index.
    ISBN 0-89079-667-X
    1. Attention-deficit hyperactivity disorder. 2. Attention-deficit hyperactivity disorder—Case studies. I. Title.
RJ506.H9N48   1995
362.1'9892589—dc20   94-41588
                                            CIP

Production Manager: Alan Grimes
Production Coordinator: Karen Swain
Art Director: Lori Kopp
Reprints Buyer: Alicia Woods
Editor: Irene Aldrich
Editorial Assistant: Claudette Landry

Printed in the United States of America

1 2 3 4 5 6 7 8 9 10   99 98 97 96

To Brian,
who has
come
so far.

Contents

Preface

Attention-Deficit/Hyperactivity Disorder (ADHD) is a relatively newly recognized syndrome. Past labels, such as Minimal Brain Dysfunction, have been discarded as new information is gathered.

Though the labeling is new, the symptoms and effects of the disorder have no doubt been affecting human lives for centuries. Our generation is the first to understand the symptoms and ramifications of living with the disorder. In the past, those who were hyperactive, impulsive, and distractible were often the school dunces, the social outcasts, the wanderers. I believe many were also our inventors, our artisans, our explorers.

The schools of the past provided restless, distractible students the structure that they needed to get through. Those who could not "make it" in school were able to quit and work at jobs that did not require a great deal of organization and attentiveness. Farm laborers, household helpers, and even small business owners could succeed without having high skill levels.

But today's society puts great demands on individuals to excel in school and in their careers and personal lives. "High tech" industry demands that workers be learned, proficient, and organized. Those qualities are very difficult for an individual with Attention-Deficit/Hyperactivity Disorder to achieve. As Russell Barkley (1993), noted psychologist and author, has said, "Our society values judgment, delay [in gratification] . . . everything that [those with ADHD] can't do or do differently."

It is my hope that parents, clinicians, and educators across our country and around the world become better informed about the specifics of ADHD and that they accept its existence, understand its difficulties, and learn to deal with it in those individuals with ADHD whom they encounter.

While common symptoms and characteristics exist within the population with ADHD, no two individuals are the same. True to human nature, each has his or her own sets of strengths and weaknesses.

This book centers on the personal story of my and my husband's struggles to understand and help our son Brian. It is intended to add the human element to the bevy of statistics already published on ADHD. Many stories will seem a mirror image of other children with ADHD; some are as unique as Brian himself.

I have neither spared the heartaches nor exaggerated them. It is my hope that by sharing our story, the reader will become more aware of the impact Attention-Deficit/Hyperactivity Disorder can have, not only on the afflicted individual but also on his or her family and anyone else in close contact with that person. I pray that this heightened awareness will affect the population with ADHD, youngsters and adults alike, in a positive way by offering them more understanding, support, and opportunity for success in their everyday lives.

For simplicity, when I refer to a child with ADHD other than Brian, I use the word *he* generically. It could almost always mean *he* or *she*.

And so, in a general way, this book goes out to all those with ADHD, whom Dr. Dale Jordan (1988) referred to as "precious strugglers" (p. v.).

Acknowledgments

Credit and thanks are due to the many who made this book possible:

To my editor and mentor, Margaret Larson, who made revisions without changing my style.

To Tamara Cook for her computer skills and artwork.

To all my family, especially Mary, Jane, Donna, and Joe, and to my many friends for their invaluable interest, suggestions, and support.

To Dr. Denyse Olson-Dorff, Psy.D., whose personal yet professional care gives us hope in dark moments.

To my mother and my deceased father, whose examples taught me to love unconditionally and to strive for the best within each of us.

To my sons, Brad, Brian, and Craig, who put up with all the hours of Mom glued to the computer "writing her book."

And to my husband, Mark, who kept the house and kids going while I wrote and rewrote. And mostly for his willingness to reach out with me and pursue the journey into a world once unfamiliar to us—that of Attention-Deficit/Hyperactivity Disorder.

Meet Brian

Sweet, cuddly, intelligent, witty. Hyperactive.

Brian's birth could only be described as "fast and furious." Yet, as an infant, Brian was fairly mellow. He seemed a welcome contrast to his older brother, Brad, who had been energetic from day one and walked and talked well before his first birthday.

Though this second son was more physically content, he was demanding in his own way. Brian definitely did not let me (his mother) sleep much! He insisted on being fed every 2 to 2½ hours and was nearly 6 months old before he slept all night. Although Brian was very alert, he was not active in a typical way. He crawled far less than most babies and did not walk alone until nearly 16 months.

Through his 2nd year, Brian was often content to sit in one spot and play a single activity for quite a while. He was good at playing alone. Brian was especially fond of toys with many small parts and would play with them endlessly. Often his play consisted of throwing books, emptying drawers, or disassembling toys, though he had neither the desire nor the ability to reconstruct even the simplest ones.

By the time Brian was 2 years old, his behavior began to worry Mark and me. They were typical 2-year-old things, but somehow they seemed more intense, and definitely more constant. While most 2-year-olds will stop whining or hitting when a parent firmly tells them to, Brian never did. He rarely responded to repeated requests or even to discipline, such as being sent to a different

1

room. Rewards (e.g., crackers) could not entice him to listen to us or to change his actions.

He would awake by 6:00 a.m. and come bounding into our bedroom and climb in, not *with* us, but *on top* of us. He would wiggle and bounce and do his best to annoy Mark and me. Brian loved to put his fingers and feet in our faces, not to mention his smelly, diapered bottom!

Putting him out of the bed would stop him momentarily, but as soon as he was allowed back in, he would start all over. He'd giggle and squirm and poke us some more. Brian seemed to delight in annoying us. Mark and I began to take turns getting up with him immediately so the other could stay in bed. We could never lie with him and snuggle, even if I tried to calm him with a story or song. It was not a pleasant way to start each day.

Over the next 2 years, other behaviors surfaced that continued to concern us. Brian was often rude, whiny, aggressive, uncooperative, and just plain frustrating to us. Our oldest son, Brad, had always been a challenge (certainly not the laid-back type), but somehow Brian was different. Some days he scared me, the way he seemed driven to extremes.

I began to read books on raising a difficult child. Mark and I toyed with thoughts of allergy testing and chiropractic treatment. Calls to these professionals told me that they probably could not help. I consulted Brian's pediatrician, who noted our concerns but found nothing unusual. (Of course, Brian was usually cooperative as can be when in her office!)

By now, Brian's conduct was becoming apparent to neighbors, extended family, and others. My parents, siblings, and I got together as often as the miles allowed. I began to dread our gatherings because of Brian's noisy and irritating behavior, which disturbed everyone, especially at mealtime. Inevitably I would end up removing Brian from the table and then leaving in tears of my own frustration.

Brian frequently pestered his brother Brad, who now responded with aggression of his own. Mark and I were constantly pulling them apart.

Mark and I began to disagree on how to discipline Brian. I was not happy with his behavior but felt Mark was expecting too much for a 3-year-old. Mark felt I was too easy on him. Looking back, both statements were probably correct to a point, but for the most part we were doing OK. A family of two tired, working parents with two young boys can be a strain in itself; we had the added worry of what, if anything, was wrong with our son.

I like to read and continued to search for an answer. Mark and I considered every approach imaginable, but we were careful to use each method long enough to be consistent and not to be constantly changing our expectations of him. My cumulative feeling was one of increasing concern, frustration, and fear.

Mark was also concerned, but because of my more searching, assertive personality, I was the one to pursue. For a time it was a driving force in me to find an answer and help Brian. There were weeks when I was consumed by the need to resolve this problem. His conduct and our reactions to it were not doing good things for our family life.

My family and close friends were sympathetic, but they never really saw how severe Brian's actions could be. The only "outside" person who had really experienced the spectrum of Brian's behavior was my mother, who at times spent a day or two caring for the boys.

My older sister, Jane, worked with children with special learning disabilities, so I had discussed Brian's behavior with her. But this was mostly unproductive; because she lived in Hawaii and we in Wisconsin, she had not seen Brian often or long enough to evaluate his behavior.

Preschool (2 half-days a week) was not going well, and mornings were a disaster. Brian was now showing some disturbing behaviors. He would wake up (still early) and run down the hall, often literally bouncing off the walls. He would bang into the wall, fling up his arms, and bounce himself backward, then bump into the opposite wall.

In the fall when Brian was 5 years 3 months old, my sister spent a week at home with our mother. I hoped Jane would give me her ideas on the continuing problem. After spending an hour or so at our house, I asked whether she had noticed Brian's unusual behaviors. Though he had been relatively "good," she had noticed. Jane asked whether I had heard of "ADD," Attention-Deficit Disorder. I had not, so she explained it briefly to me.

Attention-Deficit Disorder: It seemed a pretty clear, descriptive title. I thought it meant short attention span. But Brian could sit for long periods and play by himself and would have sat and watched TV for hours if we had let him. So I didn't think that Brian had a problem with attention, but I was willing to check it out.

She also mentioned hyperactivity. I thought of a child who runs around, racing from room to room, terrorizing the grocery store—a child who never stops. Now Brian was busy and did create a lot of havoc, but not in that way. So I really wasn't sure that this disorder fit Brian, but I was willing to check this out, too.

Jane had taught children with this disorder and told me that many took medication, usually Ritalin, to help them in school. I have never cared for medicines unless they were absolutely necessary, so this idea did not appeal to me. Others had several times suggested medication, but I had always refused to consider "sedating" my son. Yet Mark and I were becoming desperate. Jane felt sure that Brian showed at least some signs of ADD and should be tested by a professional. I am eternally grateful for her accurate observation and her urging me to consult a doctor.

We then learned of more aspects of Attention-Deficit/ Hyperactivity Disorder (ADHD); these did, indeed, sound like Brian. Now that we knew what ADHD was, Mark and I had a purpose to our searching, and, possibly, an explanation for Brian's troubles. Thus began our long, often difficult, but eventually rewarding process of discovering for ourselves what Attention-Deficit/Hyperactivity Disorder really means and how to live with it.

Explaining ADHD 2.

Attention-Deficit/Hyperactivity Disorder (ADHD) is a combination of symptoms, *not* a single disease. There are two schools of thought—one states that hyperactivity is an inherent part of the disorder, which is always termed ADHD. Others feel that there are two forms of the disorder: ADHD (with hyperactivity) and ADD (without).

Each child with ADHD is different, but some of the common characteristics of the disorder are listed below:

Hyperactivity or restlessness

Impulsivity (responds quickly without considering alternatives, interrupts, has difficulty waiting turns, engages in risky behavior)

Noncompliance/resistance to discipline

Social and emotional immaturity

Poor organizational skills

Aggressiveness

Difficulty with transitions

Daydreams, is "spacey," easily confused

Difficulty with sequential activities and cause-and-effect relationships

Low frustration threshold

Skeptics will point out that most of these characteristics are normal childhood behaviors, which is true, but the child with ADHD exhibits them in a much more con-

stant and extreme fashion than is normal. The behaviors'
severity and constancy over time are included in the
diagnostic criteria for the disorder.

Attention-Deficit/Hyperactivity Disorder is defined by
the *Diagnostic and Statistical Manual of Mental Disorders*
(4th ed.), published in 1994 by the American Psychiatric
Association, known as DSM-IV. These official criteria,
listed below, describe in more detail than past DSMs the
symptoms of ADHD (with hyperactivity) and also of ADD
(without hyperactivity) and suggest how the disorder can
affect adults.

**Diagnostic criteria for Attention-Deficit/Hyper-
activity Disorder**

A. Either (1) or (2):

(1) six (or more) of the following symptoms of inattention have persisted for at least 6 months to a
degree that is maladaptive and inconsistent with
developmental level:

Inattention

(a) often fails to give close attention to details or
makes careless mistakes in schoolwork, work,
or other activities

(b) often has difficulty sustaining attention in
tasks or play activities

(c) often does not seem to listen when spoken to
directly

(d) often does not follow through on instructions
and fails to finish schoolwork, chores, or
duties in the workplace (not due to oppositional behavior or failure to understand
instructions)

(e) often has difficulty organizing tasks and
activities

(f) often avoids, dislikes, or is reluctant to
engage in tasks that require sustained mental effort (such as schoolwork or homework)

(g) often loses things necessary for tasks or activities (e.g., toys, school assignments, pencils, books, or tools)

(h) is often easily distracted by extraneous stimuli

(i) is often forgetful in daily activities

(2) six (or more) of the following symptoms of hyperactivity-impulsivity have persisted for at least 6 months to a degree that is maladaptive and inconsistent with developmental level:

Hyperactivity

(a) often fidgets with hands or feet or squirms in seat

(b) often leaves seat in classroom or in other situations in which remaining seated is expected

(c) often runs about or climbs excessively in situations in which it is inappropriate (in adolescents or adults, may be limited to subjective feelings of restlessness)

(d) often has difficulty playing or engaging in leisure activities quietly

(e) is often "on the go" or often acts as if "driven by a motor"

(f) often talks excessively

Impulsivity

(g) often blurts out answers before questions have been completed

(h) often has difficulty awaiting turn

(i) often interrupts or intrudes on others (e.g., butts into conversations or games)

B. Some hyperactive-impulsive or inattentive symptoms that caused impairment were present before age 7 years.

C. Some impairment from the symptoms is present in two or more settings (e.g., at school [or work] and at home).

D. There must be clear evidence of clinically significant impairment in social, academic, or occupational functioning.

E. The symptoms do not occur exclusively during the course of a Pervasive Developmental Disorder, Schizophrenia, or other Psychotic Disorder and are not better accounted for by another mental disorder (e.g., Mood Disorder, Anxiety Disorder, Dissociative Disorder, or a Personality Disorder).

Hyperactivity

The frequent, some days almost constant, wiggle-jiggle-poke-and-prod makes it difficult for other people to be with the hyperactive child. Nothing is done at a slow or uniform pace. Little is said in a moderate voice. There is a constant drive to be moving.

The obviously hyperactive child can best be described by using superlatives; he is apt to be the loudest, fastest, bounciest, most wiggly child around. He loves to run, jump, thump, jerk, bump, shriek, and scream. As Russell Barkley (as cited in Fowler, 1992) has stated, they are "behaviorally disinhibited . . . they behave too much! They are constantly interacting with their environment. Rules lose every time; those with ADHD are managed by the moment" (p. 7).

Most children will run and shout on the playground; here it is often difficult to distinguish which of the children are, indeed, hyperactive. But when those children are brought inside and guided into quiet, regulated activities indoors, the hyperactive child finds it difficult or impossible to slow down. Transitions such as these are very difficult for a child with ADHD. He is often unable to control his activity and act appropriately in situations such as classrooms, club meetings, other group gatherings, or even a family meal. A clinically hyperactive child shows an ongoing pattern of activity that is significantly more than what is displayed by his peers.

Impulsivity contributes to the appearance of hyperactive behavior. Those with ADHD "are managed by the moment," explained Dr. Barkley (1993); they have a "narrow window on time"—they want everything NOW. If a person is busy reacting, his mind cannot problem solve, cannot anticipate the results of his actions.

A typical child with ADHD will blurt out what's on his mind; he'll interrupt and push and shove to be first in line. Professor Sydney Zentall (1993) addressed the issues for children and adults with the disorder and summed it up like this: "They hate to wait!" They are never satisfied, always searching, seeking the stimulation that Zentall feels is biologically driven. Of those who are diagnosed with ADHD, 70 to 90% are of the hyperactive-impulsive type.

Hyperactivity will typically lessen as the child with ADHD enters adolescence, but his impulsivity remains or increases. He is thus even more likely to engage in risk-taking behavior than the average teenager.

Some children with ADHD are not obviously hyperactive but are squirmy, restless, and unsettled. They shift from one activity to the next, leaving a trail of clutter behind them. They are never satisfied, always searching.

Still others' minds wander endlessly, though they show few outward signs of hyperactivity. Instead, they are often slow to start, and once in an activity, they become overfocused and must be pried away from their tasks. They appear to be "spacey" and daydreaming. Yet, an unsettling sense of inner restlessness usually pervades their lives. Of those who are diagnosed with ADHD, 15 to 30% are of the inattentive type, with few or no outward signs of hyperactivity.

Attention Deficits

Attention deficits involve much more than just short attention span. It seems contradictory that a child with an attention deficit could overfocus, but he can indeed attend to something of high interest for a long time. If the task or subject is not interesting to the child, he is not being stimulated enough to sustain his attention. He may appear to not be caring or trying, but for a child with ADHD, sustained attention only occurs as long as his need for stimulation is being met.

A child with ADHD can also have difficulties with selective attention; he doesn't know which stimulus is important at what time. This difficulty with selective attention can be especially problematic in school, where the student must judge which parts of the lecture or the homework are most important. Those who are highly distractible are drawn to other more interesting stimuli and thus away from the original task. Parents and teachers must then continually draw the child's attention back to the task at hand. Richard LaVoie (1993) explained: "The distractible child pays attention to everything. The child with poor attention span pays attention to almost nothing."

A child with attention deficits often appears to be daydreaming, as if "nobody's home." He is lost in a fog, in his own world—certainly not all the time, but these "spacey" times come and go with no apparent rhyme or reason. It is easy for parents and teachers to blame the child for not listening or not trying, which is actually out of the child's control. The child with an attention deficit is following his inner self wherever it leads him.

Short attention span has its advantage—most of these children don't hold a grudge, even against those who spank them and yell and complain about their behavior. It is truly a gift to us parents that these children are very forgiving.

Most children with ADHD also have other physical, emotional, or learning difficulties, which complicate our understanding and treatment of the child. Sleep disturbances, asthma, and being accident-prone are common, as are speech and language problems and specific learning disabilities. The presence of impulsivity and hyperactivity is magnified in those who develop Oppositional/ Defiant Disorder and Conduct Disorders. According to Dr. Sam Goldstein (1993), 85% of those with ADHD also have coexisting conditions, which may include depression, obsessive-compulsive disorders, Tourette's syndrome, and/or anxiety disorders. In short, the presence of ADHD puts a child at high risk for other problems.

How common are these attention deficits and hyperactivity? The behaviors of a child with ADHD are more severe and constant than 95% of his peers. Therefore, 1 child in about 20 has ADHD. Boys are three to six times more likely than girls to be diagnosed as being hyperactive and having attention deficits.

The cause of ADHD cannot yet be singled out in any certain child. There are several possible causes; it can be from a lack of oxygen before or during birth or toxins or other complications during pregnancy, though cases with these causes are thought to be few. Recent research, especially in genetics, has strongly suggested that ADHD is usually inherited. One-half to two-thirds of youths with ADHD have another family member with the disorder. Thus, many families with one child having the disorder will find that a sibling also has ADHD, or one of the parents discovers that it has been the source of his (or her) own life struggles with work, school, or relationships.

I was an extremely active child and would probably be considered a hyperactive adult. I have always felt driven to accomplish and create, and so most of my energies have been routed into productive pursuits. Only now, in my late 30s, am I comfortable with just sitting still—now and then.

Attention-Deficit/Hyperactivity Disorder cannot be caused by "poor" parenting. A child's parents and environment can contribute to his overall conduct, but they cannot actually cause the clinical disorder.

There is much ongoing research to find the cause of ADHD. Symptoms of the disorder seem to be caused by a dysfunction in processes governing alertness and communication feedback. Especially for those without hyperactivity, problems may stem from underarousal of certain brain functions. Whatever the exact cause (or possible combination of causes) individuals with ADHD are neurobiologically different.

It is known that the frontal brain activity in individuals with ADHD is impaired. In 1990 Dr. Alan Zametkin published results of a PET-scan study on adults with ADHD. The brain activity in those individuals was definitely different from the brain activity of "normal" (nondisordered) adults. Surprisingly to most, the adults with ADHD showed *lower* activity in the frontal lobe, which suggests a less than normal ability to control activities and impulses. Studies by numerous researchers are documenting other neurobiological links to attention deficits and hyperactivity.

Dr. Barkley (1993) believes that ADHD is a motivational deficit, not for want of trying but for lack of *ability* to motivate. The child with ADHD does not respond well to rules, though he needs them to stay on track and must be reminded and reinforced continually. This task is one of the most frustrating responsibilities of parenting a child with ADHD. He cannot help the way he is. He is naturally disorganized, inconsistent, and impulsive. However, he can be taught to control these symptoms to minimize his difficulties and live a relatively normal life.

Without guidance, children with ADHD become lonely, confused, scorned, and often depressed. They have extremely low self-esteem. Many of them act on their frustrations with aggression or defiance.

There are varying degrees of the disorder; it occurs along a continuum. Some children can function well in school and at home with proper supervision and guidance. Many individuals continue to struggle even when receiving ongoing medical and psychological treatment.

It was once thought that most children with ADHD outgrow their symptoms during puberty. This knowledge was often my bit of light at the end of our tunnel. But recent research (Barkley, 1993) has suggested that 80% are still attention deficit in adolescence, and at least 50% into adulthood.

Literature from our clinic (Department of Behavioral Medicine, Gundersen Clinic, n.d.) stated: "Hyperactivity is often outgrown but ADHD children rarely outgrow problems with attention and concentration. These difficulties follow them through the teen years; some continue to have significant problems throughout their adult lives."

One key to success is to evaluate and deal with the problem while the child is young and to continue treatment. Parents and teachers can then work with and guide the child. The goal is that by the time he reaches his teens, he should be fairly well under control and have developed good social and organizational habits. He'll have learned how to work around his problems and be able to manage difficult situations; his self-esteem will remain high.

As with any child, parents can only do their best. Mark and I try to give Brian and his brothers as much love, encouragement, and support as we can. We hope they will be able to take it from there and lead loving, positive, and productive lives.

Brian's Awareness 3.

Brian has always been more acutely aware of what was going on within himself than most children with ADHD are. From an early age he has used expressions to describe his feelings, both physical and emotional, in a way that is unique and perceptive beyond his years.

At age 3, especially when given two or more instructions, Brian often would shake his head, give a puzzled look, and say, "I get all scribbly." This phrase became his way of expressing confusion or lost thought processes. It was spoken most frequently when we gave directions, such as "Bring me your shoes" or "Clean up your toys." The "scribbly" feeling seemed to be an overused excuse, and we eventually tended to ignore it. Yet instinct told me he did get "scribbly," and, as more of his disorder revealed itself, I realized how accurate his early expression was.

Another "excuse" was, as he put it, "My tummyache hurts." Every child develops stomachaches at opportune times. Looking back, I believe Brian used these excuses like any other child to avoid work or an activity he didn't care for. What we could not know, however, until years later, is that he at times had very legitimate aches.

Dr. Dale Jordan (1992) wrote: "[ADHD] children cannot ignore intrusions into their sensory awareness" (p. 7). They will often notice sounds, odors, and physical sensations well before others. The story *Eagle Eyes* (Gehret, 1991) points out how these abilities can be advantageous.

But many children are tactilely sensitive to a point of discomfort. It is not uncommon for them to be bothered by things that most people never notice, such as the rubbing caused by labels on a shirt and the seams of socks. When tired, their sensitivity increases.

Sensitivity to Light

Brian's stomachaches, combined with a sensitivity to light, were actually early signs of migraine headaches. I'd always accepted the light factor as real rather than an excuse; I'm glad now that I did believe him.

Brian has never liked strong lights or sunshine. I can still hear him complain at age 2 or 3, "The sun hurts my eyes." Recently I spoke with two of his early baby-sitters. When I mentioned his headaches and aversion to lights, they both recalled that Brian did not want to be outside in the sun.

Brian has always preferred to play in the house, even on glorious summer days, which sometimes irritated me. I thrive on fresh air and sunshine, so I naturally preferred to see him outside also. But staying inside actually was, to him, a retreat from this uncomfortable sensation.

I tried to accept Brian's reluctance to be in the bright sun. I often suggested an activity in the shade to lure him outside at all. Both Mark and I made sure he did not get too much sun, as he overheated easily and we feared sunstroke.

When Brian was 7, we had his eyes examined by an optometrist, who noticed Brian's extreme sensitivity to light. He recommended a pair of polarized, nonprescription sunglasses. When Brian first put on the new "shades," he grinned broadly and said, "This is how I want my world to look!"

Sensitivity to Sound

The best example of Brian's acute sense of sound comes from my memory of being in the kitchen with him when he was 3 or 4 years old. He was at the table, looking at books. I was preparing to wash dishes and turned on the faucet. He got very excited and shouted, "Shut that up!" I turned the faucet off, and he settled down. In a minute I turned on the tap again—same reaction.

I realized then that he'd been telling all of us to "shut up" lately. I did not like his choice of words, but he continued to demand quiet. We observed carefully for a time and noticed Brian would become upset at voices or sounds even from the next room while he was trying to concentrate on an activity.

Brian has had routine auditory tests plus one extra at my request after his preschool teacher wondered several times whether he heard well. Since that test was normal, we assumed he was not paying attention well or he was ignoring what was being said.

Teachers and parents of children with attention deficits commonly think their children are ignoring instructions, but the children actually cannot process the oral messages properly. It took us a while to determine that Brian's problem was related to an inability to process the information rather than an inability to hear.

Brian at age 5 was still too young for a central auditory processing test, which determines if messages he hears get lost or "jumbled" en route to the brain. We have not since had Brian tested for auditory processing because of expense and, more important, because nothing could be done to physically cure a problem if it were found.

In the following years Brian had scattered periods of noises making him especially uncomfortable. One day he went to the school sickbed complaining of headache and earache. A rest and aspirin helped him make it through the rest of the day. When I picked him up after school, he told me that he liked the office because "the loudest it gets there is number 1 on the Richter scale." In his own clever way, he was telling me that the office is quiet and comfortable compared to his classroom.

Several weeks later Brian still complained of noisiness almost daily. Then he added the complaint of an earache. He showed no other symptoms, so I waited 2 days to take him to the clinic. The doctors found nothing amiss. Two days later Mark took him in again: same complaint, same lack of diagnosis. I explained to Brian the difference between earache and bothersome noises, but he continued to be disturbed. He obviously was having much trouble coping with noises. Later that same month, he explained in his own words: "My head and ears and eyes are so sensitive. Sounds that come into my ears get louder before they hit my eardrums."

Interestingly enough, his own voice was usually loud even though he preferred others to speak softly. The first time my sister mentioned his loud voice, I was surprised she thought so. But when I thought about it, Brian was loud; we had just grown used to his decibel level.

Conversation can get boisterous in a house with three boys (and a talkative mother), but even at normal levels he still sometimes claps his hands over his ears and asks us to "shut up because it hurts my ears."

Brian's Observations

I have never been able to link his days and weeks of increased sensitivity to anything in particular. He does exhibit several disturbances at these times. When the attention-deficit symptoms show up, they do so in clusters, and it is obvious Brian is having a hard time.

On some days Brian seems at the mercy of his environment. Every sight and sound distracts him. I can speak directly to him and he does not hear; his eyes are flitting around the room, catching every motion or any object at all. The disorder causes his attention to be easily drawn *to* outside stimuli, consequently drawing his attention *away* from the task at hand, thus the term *attention deficit*.

I've been reminded in seminars about the demands placed on children with ADHD by the world. The demands are the same as any other person has, but the children with ADHD cannot deal with them as easily. It sheds a new light on understanding these children when we think of everyday sounds, sights, and contacts as being extraordinarily upsetting.

It is likely a child with ADHD could be distracted or disturbed by physical contact with another person, even if that contact is meant to be nonthreatening or even nurturing. I have read of and spoken to mothers who've said that even as babies, their children with ADHD did not care to be cuddled or held much. I'm thankful that Brian has loved cuddling and hugging, though usually only at his own asking.

Brian often misinterprets actions by the rest of us, vehemently shaking off a hand on his arm, for example. Even if it was placed there kindly, he may still find it threatening, irritating, and upsetting. That action, no matter how well intended, was a real intrusion into his sensory awareness.

Brian was 3 when one day he described a feeling to Mark and me. I can still see him standing in the kitchen as we listened in awe. He ran his finger across the top of his head in a line from the crown to the center of the forehead. He then told us that he has two sides to his brain. "This side of my brain makes me be good and that side makes me be bad." I know now that he was expressing confusion over why he often misbehaved when he was truly trying not to.

Periodically through the years he has resorted to that concept of a divided brain, only not always in reference to the "good" and "bad" sides. Brian's comments were always unprompted and spontaneous. They showed how aware he was of himself and his inner struggle.

After school one day when Brian was in the second grade, he told me, "My brain is all mixed up like it's opposite day." This was Brian's way of saying he felt confused, as if he couldn't think straight. And one evening he said, "My brain makes the rest of my body do things it doesn't want to," and he demonstrated his arm trying to hit something or someone. What a struggle for a young one to go through!

When Brian suffered from frequent headaches early in the second grade, he laid his head on the pillow one night, clutched his head, and told me that it "was cracking open." During this same period, when sunlight was disturbing, he said that "the sun drills a hole in my eyes." Brian's ability to express himself has helped us understand him and has given doctors a clearer picture of what was going on.

Despite the acute awareness of what is going on within himself, Brian is not usually aware of what is going on outside. This unawareness is one of the ironies of children with attention deficits; they are surprisingly oblivious to others' reactions to them. Brian's doctor explained that they do not catch on to social cues. Most children learn proper social behaviors by trial and error, thus changing or eliminating certain behaviors after adverse reactions from others. The child with ADHD just plain does not catch on. He will repeat the offensive behavior again and again, even after being shunned or told not to do it.

For example, Brian would run up to another child on the playground and shake and wiggle his hands in the child's face. He was then surprised and offended when the other child pushed him away or avoided him the next time. Brian did not understand the connection between his initial action and the classmate's reaction. He was truly unaware of what feelings he had caused in the other child. Because of his ADHD, Brian cannot completely process information that would seem obvious to most of us. He just doesn't catch on.

Perhaps the inability of children with ADHD to understand the connection between their actions and others' reactions is why many of their parents complain that their children blame others for their own troubles and do not seem to learn from their mistakes. Even an older person with ADHD often does not understand what effect his actions are having on others. I've also heard similar comments from spouses of individuals with ADHD.

In spite of his inner awareness, Brian, like the typical child with ADHD, is unknowingly a victim of his own behavior.

Development of 4. Children with ADHD

Motor Skills

Our first son, Brad, crawled at 7 months and was walking everywhere by 11 months. Brian did very little crawling as an infant. He began to creep at 8 months; at nearly 11 months he was just beginning to crawl and didn't walk until he was over 15 months old. We have tried to avoid making comparisons between our first two sons and with our third as well, but it was impossible not to notice Brian's slow development. Brian's skills came later than average but not later than normal, which is an important distinction.

Not every child with ADHD has developmental delays. Many of those children who are also hyperactive achieve mobility—walking, running, and climbing—much earlier than average. These youngsters are often referred to as "curtain climbers." Many of them are also heedless of danger. Even when old enough to know the hazards of their activities, they proceed recklessly and thus are accident-prone.

Some children with ADHD are late to develop fine motor skills, such as tying shoelaces or using a pair of scissors or a pencil. According to the teacher's text *Who Am I in the Lives of Children?* (Feeney et al., 1991), a typical 2- to 4-year-old "explores and manipulates materials ... tries to discover ... color, texture, tools, and techniques." The scribbling stage is defined as ages 2 to 3. I was a bit concerned that Brian, at nearly 4, took no interest in drawing or coloring, and, when he did so, that his attempts were mere scribbles. Trying to control a pencil was quite frustrating for Brian, and I had not yet been able to get him to use a pair of scissors.

I would encourage new activities but not push him. His artistic ability makes no difference to me, but creative processes are part of a person's overall development; I did want to keep track of where Brian was heading.

I was eager for Brian to have the school district's routine preschool screening. We suspected he had some special needs and felt he would benefit socially from structured activity with others his age. Brian had not yet had a regular playmate, nor had he shown any interest in reaching out beyond our family for companionship. Brian also had some speech difficulties, which I hoped could be improved in preschool.

The day of the preschool testing, we took one step into the room, and Brian began to wail. We called his older brother out of class, and, with Brad at his side, Brian now finished easily enough. His test scores for communication skills and grasp of concepts were fairly high. His gross motor skills showed moderately high, except for hopping and skipping, which require balance and coordination. The low scores were, not surprisingly, in fine motor skills.

The person testing him reported that in holding the pencil he had a "poor grip." The actual reproductions of his attempts at copying shapes are shown in Figure 4.1.

If we had known then that we were dealing with a specific disorder, he probably would have qualified for the preschool program, or I could have insisted that he be admitted. But at the time, none of us were aware of the presence of ADHD. There were few spots available, and those filled with children of more apparent needs.

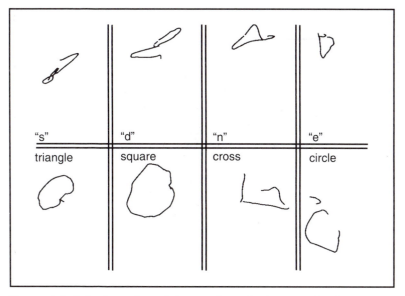

Figure 4.1. Brian's copies of shapes done during preschool testing.

Therefore we enrolled Brian in a private preschool. There he drew his first true picture with a purpose; that is, he intentionally set up to portray a certain object: a forest (see Figure 4.2). The shapes are simple—no leaves or branches—but he purposely used a green crayon and drew what he had set out to draw. This drawing was a small accomplishment but one that made me rest easier for a time. Interestingly, his concept of "a forest" rather than simply "trees" was far ahead of his physical portrayal.

Brian's drawings remained simplistic throughout kindergarten and first grade. I noticed this and discussed it with his teachers; they weren't concerned. Brian was usually in a hurry to do any project and was not one to put in extra effort, especially when it involved drawing. But when given a choice between drawing or writing in his first-grade journal, Brian preferred to draw. His simple

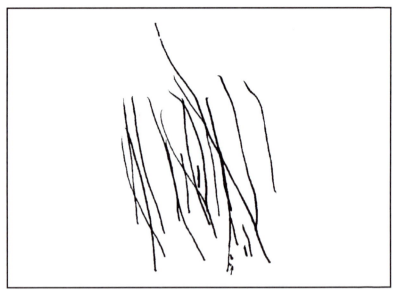

Figure 4.2. Drawing of a forest by Brian at 4¹/₂ years.

drawings were easier for him than forming each letter. Even then, his concepts were more sophisticated than his penciling abilities, which lagged far behind.

Brian struggled to learn to print the alphabet. Even at age 7 he did not print most of the letters clearly or consistently. Upon learning to write "cursive" (script writing rather than printing), his skills were fine. Brian's printing skills were well below average for his grade; his cursive characters were average or above. Brian did the characters in Figure 4.3 within 2 weeks of each other. They show the difference between his mastery of cursive and his attempts at printing.

I believe cursive was easier because in printing, each letter is a series of separate pencil strokes. Lifting the pencil off the paper after every small motion was disconcerting and hard for Brian to follow. Cursive is a continuous unbroken motion; Brian was successful at it because his thought process was also unbroken.

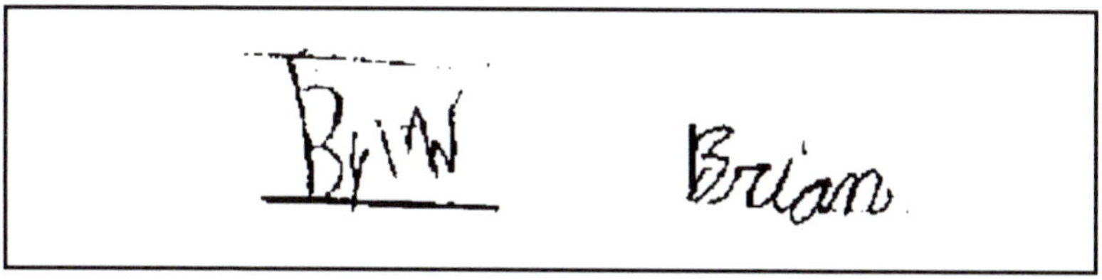

Figure 4.3. Example of Brian's printing and cursive.

By mid-second grade, Brian showed sudden, great improvement and interest in coloring and other art-related activities. We have found that in many areas in which he has been lagging, progress seems to come suddenly and he catches up to his classmates in a short time.

One second-grade project was drawing a map of an imaginary land. Brian usually put off assignments, especially when they involved drawing. It was already late in the evening when he tuned in and started detailing the map. Mark, Brad, and I were watching quietly and from a distance. We exchanged looks of surprise and awe. His drawing was much better and more detailed than usual. We were all proud of the results; that map stayed on display in our kitchen for quite some time.

I have wondered if part of his difficulty with motor activities has been that he is naturally left-handed but eats and writes right-handed. We have never forced him to use his right hand. As a toddler Brian showed a preference for his left hand. I would put a toy or spoon directly in front of him to let him choose which hand he would use to pick up the object; he usually used his right. Yet Brian approaches activities such as golfing, throwing a ball, or mounting a bicycle as a left-hander. Perhaps this mixed-hand dominance compounds his fine motor difficulties.

Brian's gross motor skills have always been normal, though slower than average to develop. As in crawling and walking, he learned to ride a bike and to swim later and with more difficulty than most of his classmates. He does have high interest and good ability in several sports; golf and baseball are his favorites.

While many children with ADHD are bright, they sometimes develop certain skills more slowly and often less fully than the average child develops. Brian's difficulty with motor skills is just one more factor in the total picture of being a child with attention deficits.

Social Development

Brian's social development has been, and continues to be, his biggest area of need. In his first few years, he had no constant playmate other than his brother Brad, who is 4 years older. Neighbor children were also at least 4 years older, and children at his daytime sitters' houses were either much younger or older.

When Brian was 2 and Brad was 6, they picked on each other and wrestled a fair amount, but I accepted it as normal sibling interaction. I also attributed their behavior to the old saying that "boys will be boys."

The first several mornings of preschool, Brian seemed shy and withdrawn—typical behavior for a young child in a new setting. He never cried or begged not to go, but as I left him each morning he began to hang back more and more. As I watched from a distance, Brian would retreat from the group and lay flat on the floor, rocking gently and looking around. I knew better than to re-enter the room, but it was so hard to leave him like that.

Our third son, Craig, was born during this time. It seemed to me that Brian was becoming more and more annoying and defiant, but we waited him out. We felt he was adjusting to many recent changes: preschool, a new brother, our move to a new house, and his grandpa's death.

We hoped it was just a stage.

I don't recall if Brian was offensive in the preschool classroom, but his aggression toward Brad at home was escalating. Brian did not try to join group activities at preschool; he often took the role of onlooker rather than participant. Yet he seemed happy enough to go there.

Mark and I discussed concerns about Brian's uncommon behaviors with his preschool teachers, but none of us could pinpoint just what his specific needs might be. One of his teachers was concerned enough to visit us at home to talk the matter over. She said in a kind but puzzled way, "I've never met a child quite like Brian." She reaffirmed my thoughts that Brian might require special attention, yet I appreciated her noticing his endearing qualities as well.

Brian's teachers questioned us about his hearing. He did not seem to hear or respond to many of their requests. At first we thought it was his way of ignoring them as he seemed to do to us at home. His defiance and non-compliance were becoming a real problem for Mark and me.

The teachers repeated their concerns. I took him to his pediatrician, who ordered an audiological test. His hearing was normal. The pediatrician talked with me about how to handle him and gave me a book, *Living with Children*, by Gerald R. Patterson (1976). His pediatrician thought he was a behavior problem; maybe with the help of the book Mark and I could handle him better. I suppose in retrospect that I could resent her assumption and that nothing more was done to discover Brian's disorder at that time. In early school and clinic testings, Brian always seemed to be on the borderline of needing special services, but he never was a strong candidate. Yet I knew he *was* special, and I continued to wonder and worry.

Brian developed a nervous habit of licking his lips often, until they were red and chapped. He also tugged at the waist of his pants every few minutes all day long.

These were repetitive, unconscious movements on his part, and I wondered what inner anxiety caused him to do them.

Brian's hyperactivity was now beginning to be obvious to others. Kindergarten brought social conflicts because of his excessive activity level and distractibility. At reading time he could hardly sit still in his space on the rug. His elbows and knees were constantly invading someone else's space. Brian seemed oblivious to his own actions but became disturbed when another child bumped him. He was frequently reprimanded for running in the hall or pushing in line.

Mark and I requested a complete evaluation of Brian through the special learning department at school. The evaluation determined he did not have specific learning disabilities but indicated concerns about his social skills and speech.

Brian was enrolled in "friendship group" sessions to help him learn how to interact with his classmates. We talked to him about the concepts discussed in his friendship group: sharing, acceptance, and cooperation. Sometimes Brian seemed sensitive to the issues; often he was scornful. He remained a loner. Brian's social development was, for years, almost stagnant.

We considered having Brian repeat second grade even though his academic skills were high. We thought it would give him time to catch up socially with his classmates, especially since he is young for his grade. I had convinced myself that this would be helpful to his social maturation.

Brian's psychologist discouraged us. She told us that our reasoning seemed clear, but repeating the grade would actually put his social development "on hold" for one more year. No matter what his chronological age, the child with ADHD will usually act less mature than his classmates do. By middle and high school, teachers and parents expect the child to catch up and grow up, but the adolescent with ADHD will usually still act younger than his age in many ways. Studies by Russell Barkley (1992) show that the individual with ADHD will remain an average of 30% behind his peers in overall development. Therefore, Brian at age 10 predictably acted more like a typical 7-year-old. Likewise, a 25-year-old young adult with ADHD may still be experiencing and living life as we'd expect of an 18-year-old.

Summers usually go well for Brian. He is content and quite happy to spend his days wandering around the house and yard doing whatever interests him at the time. Our family's summer schedule is looser and attitudes more casual; Brian thrives in it. However, those summers he spent part of his time in a day care center, he resisted the structure.

The summer before Brian entered third grade was the first time we saw him playing with Brad and having more fun than conflict. That same year, Brian made a few attempts to contact a classmate and spend an hour with him. Brian's willingness to do that was in itself a monumental step forward. Later years brought similar signs that by themselves seem insignificant but, when added to one another, cast a brighter outlook on Brian's future.

Despite this progress, Brian is still, and probably always will be, well behind his peers in social skills. A common question that parents of children with ADHD ask one another is "Does your child have friends?" Children with attention deficits are usually socially inept; lack of friends is common. Brian's lack has maybe been due less to antisocial behavior than to an absence of his reaching out to others.

Other Concerns

One day in kindergarten Brian had a seizure. It was a "petit mal," not serious. A pediatric neurologist did several tests, including an EEG (brain-wave scan). The results did not indicate further problems, but we still worried. Brian, innocent as he was, proudly showed off the graphs of his "brain test." He has since had one episode that was a possible seizure, but we are aware of no more.

Speech difficulties hindered Brian's attempts to mingle with other children. People outside our immediate family had a hard time understanding him, but Mark, Brad, and I had learned to interpret those sounds he did not say clearly. The speech clinician at his preschool testing assured me that the sounds he was struggling with were not unusual for his age.

After his special school evaluation in first grade, Brian began speech therapy two or three times a week. He made slow but steady progress throughout the second and third grades. We supplemented the school sessions the first year with summer speech therapy at our clinic.

Brian acted hurt and defensive when anyone questioned him or did not understand what he had just said. He once told me, "Mom, I say words right, but others don't hear them the way my ears do."

Another worry for us has been Brian's recurring headaches. We now know that his "tummyaches" and sensitivity to light as a toddler were early signs of cluster or migraine headaches. Seizures are sometimes related to them also.

When Brian was 6½ years old, he began telling us he was seeing "balls" in front of his eyes. He described them as having many colors and moving back and forth. These "balls" appeared suddenly and left within a minute. A children's neurologist tested Brian and questioned us extensively. He ordered another EEG—Brian's second—which also appeared normal.

Soon after, Brian also described a shivering sensation in his hands and lower arms. Back to the clinic! This time they did a magnetic resonance imaging (MRI). The MRI is a sophisticated, and expensive, means of viewing the brain cells and tissues in detail. Brian's neurologist found no reason for the "shivering," and no tumors or abnormalities were found. Now at least we could rest easier and know Brian's headaches were not serious.

I did, however, track his headaches for months, recording their frequency and intensity. They came in clusters, recurring several times daily for days at a time. During these weeks Brian was especially sensitive to light and noise. One night as he lay down to sleep, he complained, "My head hurts like a drill is putting a hole in it." Brian eventually learned to cope with the headaches and asked for aspirin only when the pain was severe.

I read that in some cases a special diet would alleviate migraines. Brian's pediatrician did not think it worth the effort to investigate. His neurologist neither encouraged nor discouraged us. But we wanted to give it a try and did our own research. Mark and I explained the diet to Brian and gave him a choice. Many of his favorite foods were on the list to avoid: oranges, bananas, yogurt, cheese, ice cream, peanut butter, raisins, hot dogs, chocolate, and a dozen others. Brian was willing to try it right away, as he said, "I'm not going to take any chances." We stayed with the diet faithfully; his headaches did diminish. Substitutes for many of the foods were available at a nearby food co-op. We were fortunate to have cooperation from the school cooks in heating food for him that I'd specially prepared. By fifth grade we slacked off on the diet; he seemed to have outgrown the headaches, for the most part.

The special diet alleviated his headaches but *not* his inattention or hyperactivity.

Most children with ADHD have multiple problems; we are constantly struggling with one or another aspect of Brian's disorder. Each day brings a new challenge—for him and for us. Little comes easily. And when things could be going well, he often creates conflict or disaster where there shouldn't be any. It is difficult for the rest of the family not to get bogged down by the struggles that every day seems to bring.

Each of our concerns about Brian is, by itself, fairly minor. But grouped together, they create quite a worry. None of Brian's medical problems is severe; I see others in the clinic waiting room so much worse off than he is. But, with Brian's difficulties in so many areas, I often look at him with a heavy heart.

Diagnosing ADHD 5.

Every bouncy, busy, or restless young child is not clinically hyperactive. Likewise, not all impulsive or inattentive children have ADHD. General conduct problems, learning disabilities, and emotional disorders can also appear to be ADHD. Careful study needs to be done by a skilled professional to obtain the correct diagnosis. That professional could be a pediatrician with expertise in ADHD, a pediatric neurologist, or a child psychiatrist or psychologist. Social workers, educators, and others are also familiar with the disorder. The most thorough, and therefore most accurate, diagnoses are made by a team of professionals who carefully examine the child and interview those persons closest to him.

Some charge that too many children are being diagnosed with ADHD; that it has become a "popular" disorder. I contest that statement because, for any child who truly has the disorder, there is nothing enviable or popular about it! The key is to carefully and thoroughly assess each child who is suspected of having ADHD. In most cases a team of professionals should assess the child's development: neurological, emotional, intellectual, and social. There are numerous childhood disorders or conditions that can pose as ADHD "look-alikes." According to DSM-IV, a differential diagnosis—which considers, but rules out, other reasons for the child's struggles—will help ensure an accurate diagnosis.

Most, but not all, children with attention deficit are hyperactive. Attention-Deficit/Hyperactivity Disorder (ADHD) is more obvious, as it draws attention to itself.

Children having attention deficits without hyper-activity are often diagnosed separately from those who are hyperactive; that diagnosis is commonly one of ADD. The student with ADD is often not disruptive and can easily be passed over and never assessed or diagnosed. He drifts along because the teacher's attention is being spent on others' more apparent needs.

School personnel are often the first to suggest evaluations for attention deficits because the school setting is where many of the problems show up. The schools can recommend testing by a specialist but should not by themselves diagnose a child as having ADHD.

Even after suggestions by other family members and teachers, it can be difficult to decide if the child's problems are severe enough to warrant professional treatment. Some well-meaning persons will give advice based solely on their reactions to the child. Others will blame the parents' approach—one is too permissive, the next too strict, or a myriad of other things the parent is "doing wrong." Still others will blame the child's attitudes ("The kid can do better if he would only try" theory).

Most parents of children with ADHD feel guilty or doubtful about their own effectiveness. Many other parents blame their children for their problems. In the process of diagnosing and counseling, parents learn to deal with these feelings. Understanding the disorder is, in itself, a big step forward in helping the child.

Many people will scoff at the idea of psychological treatment. In my own dealings with our son, most of my family and friends are supportive and even admiring of our efforts to diagnose and treat the problem. Still, I sensed that some people were thinking, "What is she making such a big deal about?" or "Isn't she capable of dealing with the situation herself?" I am not ashamed to say that no, I often am not capable. There are times I feel downright unstable.

Dr. Jordan (1992) has suggested that if a child is "clearly beyond the reach of adult leadership and ... cannot succeed socially, educationally and emotionally ... it is time to work with a doctor" (p. 101). When Brian's behavior began to affect our family and its everyday functioning and parental intervention was not improving the situation, we decided it was time to seek help.

If there is a reason to suspect ongoing problems, it is a great injustice to any struggling child and his family to not at least test for ADHD (or other disorder) and continue treatment accordingly. Many children don't fit the official diagnosis but have similar problems. They, too, need help.

Many hyperactive children will behave well in a quiet, structured, or one-on-one setting. Novel or unfamiliar situations will also often hold their attention well. I remember wishing Brian would act more like usual when we visited his pediatrician so she could see why I was so concerned, but he was usually quite cooperative.

When Brian was barely 5, his pediatrician did offer to set up an appointment with a child psychologist. I was not quite ready for that, I guess, as I did not follow through. I'm sure finances were a consideration, but we also felt we had not yet done all we could on our own. About this same time Mark and I took a course in positive parenting and started using the techniques suggested in *Living with Children* (Patterson, 1976). Most of what the book said made sense to us, and we somewhat changed our attitudes and approaches to Brian, but I cannot say we tackled the program seriously at that point. Mark and I were in the early stages of searching. We didn't expect easy answers, but we had no idea then what we would be dealing with in the next few years.

But after my sister's visit and my early readings on ADHD, I pursued the search. The more we learned and read and processed information about Brian, the more convinced we became that ADHD sounded like him.

Once we started the diagnostic process, Mark and I asked a lot of questions so that we could understand the process of diagnosing and the doctors' reasons for suggesting what they did. I never feared a misdiagnosis. The testing process was thorough and specific, which made us confident in the results.

We are fortunate to live in a city with highly specialized medical services. Some weeks we were in the clinic two or three times a week. Once we started Brian's evaluation, I was determined to follow it through until we had done all we could to help him.

There is no one simple test for Attention-Deficit/Hyperactivity Disorder. It is not a disease; it is a complicated combination of symptoms. It is crucial to understand that ADHD is much more than just a short attention span.

Brian's diagnosis of ADHD was based on several sets of professional criteria, including Conner's Revised Questionnaire and the guidelines set up by the American Psychiatric Association. At that time DSM-III-R (published in 1987) was used; the current edition is DSM-IV. (These criteria are listed in Chapter 2.) If these guidelines are carefully followed, ADHD is said to be the most reliably diagnosed of all childhood disorders. Misdiagnoses are more likely to occur when there is not a multidisciplinary assessment.

It is important to note that the symptoms listed in DSM-IV must deviate from normal childish behavior in several ways: severity, frequency, age of onset, and endurance across situations and over time.

Mark and I filled out checklists and questionnaires, some individually and some together. The questions we were asked included the following:

Does your child

Pick at things (nails, hair, clothing)

Get into more trouble than others the same age

Fail to finish things

Get easily frustrated in efforts

Have aches and pains or is accident-prone

Exhibit restlessness

Appear to be unaccepted by groups

Manipulate or threaten peers

Change moods quickly and drastically

Disturb others by teasing, provoking, or interrupting

Daydream

Have no sense of fair play

We were to answer "not at all," "some," or "very much." A good share of our answers were "very much," with a lot of "some." I recall some questions that surprised me and did not fit Brian at all; I know now that these are not typical ADHD behaviors and helped to ensure his exclusion from emotional or conduct disorders. Such a differential diagnosis is important because there are numerous childhood disorders that can pose as ADHD "look-alikes."

For many children, attention deficits are first manifested in school. Then a teacher's questionnaire should be used in addition to the parents'. Brian was not yet in school, but we gathered comments from his day care providers for information to add to his assessment process. His evaluation, at age 5, included our responses to questions on past and current problems and a medical, developmental, and family history. We found out later that there is a strong possibility that Brian's ADHD has been inherited.

Those children without severe symptoms, especially without hyperactivity, often "fall through the cracks"— they struggle in school and at home but are not obvious enough to demand special attention. These children will often go undiagnosed and may have even less chance of future success than those more severe cases who have been effectively treated.

Mark was less eager than I was to go into the counseling process, but he came along willingly. Dr. O—, a psychologist who specializes in ADHD, was great at explaining it all to us. When we met her, Mark and I were at a point of extreme stress and frustration. I cried as we shared our concerns, and she was most perceptive. I remember her looking at me and gently saying, "You're really hurting, aren't you?" Was I ever!

I could tell right away that she understood what we had been through. As living with any other situation (e.g., poverty, disease, alcoholism), a person can never truly understand without having been through it. It was wonderful to talk to someone who knew.

After our first appointment of explaining our situation and filling out evaluation forms, Dr. O— met first with Brian, Mark, and me and then with only Brian. My memories of those meetings are not clear, except that her comment "You have quite a boy there" was in a tone both admiring and foreboding.

The next time we met, she told us that she was convinced that Brian was a child with Attention-Deficit/ Hyperactivity Disorder. She explained the disorder to us, gave us written information, and described where we could go from there. Ultimately, it was our decision to go ahead with counseling and treatment. We responded immediately that we would.

I will never forget her looking directly at us and telling us that we would be seeing a lot of her over the years. That struck me deeply because I understood her meaning that this would be a long and intense process. That, too, brought tears.

The disorder is never cured. It has to be managed for the rest of the child's life. If treatment is effective, it creates positive habits for the child to carry into adulthood. But the ADHD symptoms are inherent in each individual, and outside or self-help must continue so that the disorder can be managed.

We began to look at Brian and his troublesome actions differently. I had never thought of poor attentiveness as being characteristic of Brian. He did, in fact, play alone at books or games for long periods (the key word here is "alone"). Most children with ADHD can tune in on a solo activity as if they have tunnel vision. It's when another individual enters the scene that they become distracted and distraught.

Not all of Brian's negative behaviors are due to his disorder—certainly any child is forgetful, disruptive, and disobedient at times but not to the degree and the frequency that we were experiencing.

Goldstein and Goldstein (1989) explained that the typical child with ADHD is not purposely being noncompliant. Rather, he is incompetent of following through on what is expected of him. So Brian was incompetent instead of noncompliant! When I've shared that thought with other parents, I have seen them struck with sudden understanding. Their acceptance that their child has not been misbehaving willfully is perhaps the biggest step toward helping that child.

We now saw Brian's noncompliance as a lack of following through rather than as a lack of effort or intent. Now we understood that if Brian set out to do something, he could not attend to it long enough to finish it. *Could* not instead of *would* not makes a big difference. Now the words *attention deficit* began to make sense.

Dr. Harvey Parker (1988), author and lecturer, has described the treatment of ADHD: "The four cornerstones of the treatment plan . . . include medical management, behavioral modification, educational planning, and psychological counseling" (p. 13). Dr. Parker has stated that parents react to their child's diagnosis of ADHD in one of three ways:

1. Denial: They are too frightened, too proud, or too stubborn to admit their child has this disorder. Parents will set a course of increased expectations which creates more frustration in the child. This vicious cycle of failure can send [them] spiraling downward into an abyss of discouragement.

2. Putting Up With: The parents only semi-accept the diagnosis. They waiver between acceptance, tolerance, and denial, which causes inconsistent discipline. The child in turn becomes confused and insecure; his actions will tend to take more control of the family.

3. Acceptance: The diagnosis is met with fear but some sense of relief. These parents tend to search for more information. They realize that peaks and valleys are normal. The children are generally more well adjusted. (pp. 24–26)

It is fortunate for Brian that we fit into the acceptance category. I was relieved to know exactly what we were up against and that my concerns about Brian were not all in my maternal mind. Mark may have been partly "putting up with"; he vacillated between acceptance and tolerance.

But once the diagnosis was made, Mark and I committed ourselves. We knew it would not be easy. But we finally had an answer to Brian's troubles, and we knew we had to help him and turn our family life around. With the help of Dr. O— we formed a plan and began treatment for Brian's disorder. Mark and I do not always stay on track. We do not always agree. But we have remained partners in continued efforts to help Brian.

Counseling

6.

Once Brian had been diagnosed, we began to meet with Dr. O— at least once a week for the first month, then tapered to every 2 or 3 weeks for the next few months. A few times over the next year I felt I couldn't keep going without another meeting to keep us on the right track. I've even called Dr. O— in sheer desperation, just for reassurance and guidance. She has been so supportive! We still, 7 years later, go in "as needed."

She met mostly with Mark and me, little with Brian. Because of his young age (Brian was just 5), he could not be expected to monitor his own behavior without our help. As his parents, it was up to us. Even an adolescent or adult with ADHD, when newly diagnosed, will need much guidance from supportive family and friends.

We had to modify our methods of discipline and dealing with everyday situations. Mark and I worked very hard at this, trying to do what the doctor and our worksheets suggested. This was *not* easy for us. After parenting Brian for more than 4 years and his brother for 4 years before that, we were pretty well set in our methods. In examining our approaches, we tried not to feel we had done anything wrong but that certain things needed to be adapted to Brian's personality. Any parent knows that what works for one child might not for the next. We also had discovered that, but we had not yet found much of anything that did work for Brian.

Mark and I had been drawn into a vicious cycle of negativism and shouting from sheer frustration. We often felt on the edge of sanity. We were wise enough to take turns with the boys as much as we could. I often took a short walk or drive, leaving the children with Mark when I knew I had reached my limit and was being too harsh on them. Figure 6.1 depicts the effects of untreated ADHD on a family.

I do not care to imagine how destructive ADHD would have been to Brian and his relationship to Mark, me, his brothers, and others around him. I truly think that our family would have crumbled in one way or another without the outside help we have had. As with most families, we did not start professional treatment until things were already out of control.

Each time we met Dr. O— she would work with us on a different behavior modification method. We could decide which of Brian's behaviors was most troubling to us and start with that. Our first two choices were physical aggression and noncompliance. For each approach we were given simple but explicit instructions and a sheet of written materials to support us. All sounded easy, but when dealing head-on with Brian daily even the simplest of plans was difficult to carry through.

Mark was better at following through with them than I; he is naturally more structured and consistent. I was trying hard, but I wasn't comfortable with some of the exercises. One was the reward system, which meant giving stickers or pennies or hugs for proper behavior. I resented that Brian needed to be rewarded and not just be taught to be good for its own sake. My own upbringing taught me to behave just because that was the right thing to do.

Keeping charts, recording each proper behavior, and rewarding it were also stifling my routine. While on the telephone, in the kitchen, or in the bathroom, for example, it was impossible to stop what I was doing and chart Brian's successes or failures. I hated having to constantly stop to monitor Brian's actions. I had a house to keep, a business to run, and two other children to care for. I

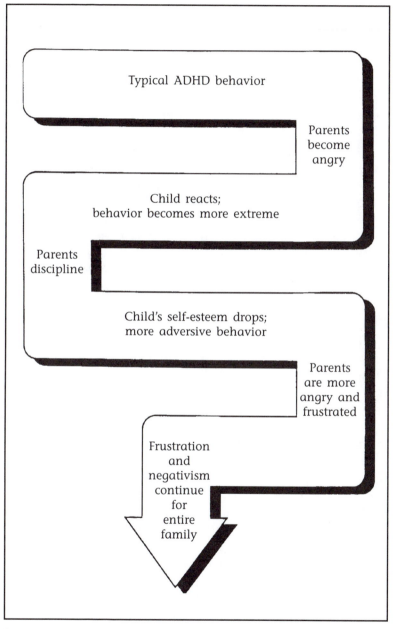

Figure 6.1. Downward-spiral effects of untreated ADHD on family.

resented the extra task of having to keep track of each occurrence. Mark did better at keeping records.

During an early counseling session, Dr. O— asked whether I was following the methods closely. I replied, "More than I am comfortable with" (and gave myself a mental pat on the back for doing so well). I did not like her response of "But that is not enough," which put even more pressure on me to conform to the methods that Dr. O— recommended. Yet I knew she meant only to help. Dr. O— firmly but gently reminded us that these children need consistency and a great deal of structure to succeed. The charts, rewards, and constant monitoring were the only effective ways to change Brian's behavior.

I'm still not crazy about the idea of rewards, but it works. When we worked on a particular behavior for a week or so, Brian would develop a habit of propriety. As this habit continued on a nearly daily basis, he would be able to continue without constant effort and reminders— the goal of any behavior modification program.

We found that we needed consistency daily but would always have to change to a new approach when the existing one showed a lack of effectiveness. Consistency was needed in *what* we expected of him, not *how* we reinforced his behavior.

"Children with attention deficits can be very challenging. Their problems . . . make daily management a difficult struggle. These children need more than the usual love, patience, and firm guidance," said the literature we got from the clinic. Do they ever!

Treating a child with ADHD takes strong commitment and much perseverance. The first step is to admit the problem and realize that something can be done to lighten the load. It may require major changes in attitudes and family routines. Resentment will be normal. It won't seem fair to devote all that extra effort to a child who has already caused so much grief.

It was hard to accept that we needed to change before Brian would. After all, we thought, he had the problem; we had been trying all along to correct it. But there must be a mutual process of change, initiated by the parents.

No matter what his age, the child with ADHD is emotionally too young to start the process of change or understand its importance. An adult must guide him into new habits and social awareness. Then the child can gradually take responsibility for his own actions.

Brian's psychologist has often encouraged Mark and me by acknowledging our cooperation and positive efforts. Those attitudes have not been easy to maintain, but we are committed to them. At times we were angry, confused, resentful, and sick and tired of having to live this way. But the choice to change was ours; the alternative of living as we had been was worse. Our efforts began to pay off.

Our hard times are much less frequent now. It is helpful that Brian's hyperactivity is lessening as he grows older. The combination of medication and management has helped him—and us—in so many ways. We still struggle with the effects of being a family coping with ADHD, but our peace of mind and pride in our progress are well worth all the effort we have put in. There are finally days, even weeks, when I feel we are a normal family after all. What a wonderful thing to finally be able to say!

It has not been easy; we have fallen off track many times. Mark and I often need to remind each other to remember what we have learned and go back to a different approach. It is so easy to fall back into the old patterns of yelling, constant reminding, and just plain giving up in exasperation. At times we still need to return to structured discipline. Every week seems to bring a different aspect of the disorder for Brian and us to deal with; his stages seem to come and go for no apparent reason.

We have taken advantage of parents' support groups as well as seminars and classes. I have read many books and pamphlets for more information and insight and keep my ears open for discussions about ADHD.

At one workshop another mother of a boy with ADHD, upon being introduced to Mark and me, quipped, "And you're still married?" I had never thought of it that way, but our struggles could certainly have created enough turmoil to split us apart. Dr. Harvey Parker (1988) has acknowledged the effects of ADHD on families: "This disorder tests the limits of most parents' patience and can easily result in marital and family stress" (p. 22). Children with ADHD often have a devastating effect on their families. Research has suggested a higher divorce rate among families with an ADHD child than those without.

CH.A.D.D., a national organization for parents of CHildren and Adults with Attention Deficit Disorder, has kept me in touch with new information in the field. As coordinator for our local CH.A.D.D. chapter, I've had the satisfaction of reaching out to and helping other parents. Affiliation with such an organization dealing with specific problems can be of great benefit to parents in understanding, effectively treating, and coping with the difficulties that they encounter.

Medical bills accompany professional help. It was a struggle to get our insurance company to approve even partial coverage for our clinic visits. Our clinic bill has a constant 4-digit dollar balance; Mark jokes that the clinic should create a column for us for money due 3 years and over. We pay consistently, and I refuse to let the bills get in the way of our children's care. Brian's health and happiness are our prime concerns, plus our family life has greatly improved since we sought professional guidance.

There are times when Mark feels I am going overboard with these sessions. Actually, I would like more, but the cost is prohibitive. Mark resents that we need all this help. I, too, wish we could do it alone. But we have to admit that we could not have come this far on our own.

I have been accused of creating excuses for Brian's misbehavior, of medicating him unjustly, and of overdoing this "thing about" ADHD. But our process of counseling and working with him has done nothing but help. No parents should be too proud to admit they need help. Anyone who cannot afford it must find a way.

Time spent on appointments, testing, and extra help for Brian at home cut even more into our already busy schedule. Once again, it was time well spent. It has been a challenge to meet Brian's special needs and still give the other boys the attention they deserve. There is little time and energy left for Mark and me to share between ourselves, not to mention the lack of time for some personal peace and quiet.

Living with a child with ADHD is, at best, a challenge and often a struggle. Having a brother with ADHD has not been easy for our other two sons. Both have had to deal with aggression and interference from Brian. His older brother, Brad, reacts with frustration and anger. The younger one, Craig, tends to strike back with aggression of his own.

For a time, Craig, then 3, showed some of the same idiosyncrasies as Brian. Not all were in imitation, because Brian had discarded some of these actions before Craig was born. Observing this and thinking we might have another son with ADHD were so frightening that I felt sheer panic. Those actions then subsided somewhat.

Brad has had a few sessions with Dr. O— to help him understand why his brother is such a "pest" and to deal with his own feelings. While we must expect Brad to do his part in keeping family harmony, I do feel bad that he is expected to put in more effort than a child his age would normally. After all, if Mark and I get sick of it, imagine how any child would feel. It is encouraging, though, to observe that their times of conflict are lessening and those of mutual play and cooperation are increasing. The boys interact pleasantly for longer periods now than I would ever have thought possible. These playtimes bring me such relief and joy!

Not even the finest professional can make ADHD go away. All the counseling in the world will not be effective unless the child's parents are willing to initiate changes at home. Counseling is meant to give parents an outlet for expression, a plan of attack, and guidance along the way. Positive efforts must come from a parent or other person working daily with the child. In our counseling for Brian, there was a certain amount of automatic therapy for Mark and me, too. I found great relief in knowing that our feelings and frustrations were normal and that I could voice them without being judged.

The counseling we have received has helped us maintain a more relaxed, much happier way of life. Mark and I have had time and space to release our frustrations and work on living in a more positive light. When we get back into our old ruts, a counseling session will reaffirm for us that we need to guide Brian as patiently as we can.

Someone who is not diagnosed until adulthood will require a great deal of counseling to break years of established habits and patterns. That same adult will respond best to treatment if a spouse, friend, or family member will guide and support him along the way.

As previously stated, part of Brian's improvement comes simply from the fact that he is older and is maturing naturally. He has learned how to behave in a more socially acceptable manner; the old aggressive actions have nearly disappeared. The combination of counseling and medication has helped develop good habits to replace the old. Yet, true to ADHD patterns, he is still less socially and emotionally mature than his peers. But by the time he'd had his 9th birthday, Mark and I looked at

Brian with pride and noticed the many ways he had grown.

There are even occasional God-sent days when we all function quite amicably. However, because most days are now "good" days, the difficult ones seem so much harder by contrast.

If there is any negative fallout from all of this effort, it is that we have nearly spent our patience and energy in the process. I've told family and friends that I honestly didn't know if I would have the stamina and strength to go through this process again. Some days I feel so burdened by thoughts of Brian and all that we struggle with. I pray for a break from the hassles. The breaks do come but never last long. Without warning, seemingly without reason, any new day might bring a new problem or an old annoyance to deal with.

Perhaps Mark and I should be more tolerant now than before we began the counseling, but these days we react more quickly and strongly to difficult situations. I feel a true sense of fright and panic when I see the old behaviors cropping up.

If all of this sounds a bit theatrical, it is not. It is real life for those of us living with a child with ADHD.

Medication

Whether or not to medicate is one of those issues that will never be agreed on by everyone. My purpose here is to share our family's experience with it.

When well-meaning family and friends suggested giving Brian medication to curb his hyperactivity, my reaction was always a vehement "no." I felt medication would be the easy way out and would only mask the problem and not help Brian learn to deal with himself. The thought was tempting at times, but we were not comfortable with doing it; Mark was even more opposed than I.

My sister who taught students with learning disabilities and had several who were "on" Ritalin said she felt they definitely benefited from it. Ritalin, though a brand name, is the commonly used term for the prescription drug methylphenidate. There are also other drugs that can be used to treat hyperactivity and attention deficits, among them dextroamphetamine (brand name Dexedrine) and, less often, pemoline (Cylert). More recently, other drugs, including some antidepressants, have been found to be helpful.

Roughly 15 to 20% of individuals with ADHD do not positively respond to medication at all. Newer drugs or combinations of drugs are beginning to help these first-time nonresponders.

Brian's pediatrician advised that using medication in combination with techniques to modify Brian's behavior would be the most effective plan. We were free to express our objections. She did not push us but did urge us to consider it.

By the time Brian was turning 5 (before his diagnosis), I began to think that medication would be an aid to what we were trying to change at home. Mark was still reluctant. Brian continued to be defiant and impulsive; Mark and I were desperate. Eventually we agreed to try medication and carefully monitor its results, if any. Brian was now 5 years 4 months old.

Brian's pediatrician prescribed the drug methylphenidate. He started on a minimal dosage of 2.5 mg in the morning and 2.5 mg again at noon. Initially we saw few changes. The school days went smoothly enough; the weekends were full of strife.

His dosage was raised to 5 mg in the morning and another 2.5 mg at noon. We now noticed an improvement in Brian's interactions with his brothers and slightly more compliance to our requests. Brian was less distractible; he could tolerate more than one conversation going on at one time. But he continued to have behavioral problems: aggression, crying, and resistance to discipline.

Brian's medication was increased over the next few weeks to 10 mg in the morning plus 5 mg at noon, but this increased dosage made him appear tired and pale. We determined immediately that it was too much, so we stopped medication until we could see a specialist. In the two weeks that followed, Mark and I felt Brian was once again more distractible, but we were not yet convinced it was due to the absence of medication.

We finally met with Dr. O—, a child psychologist, and went through a thorough evaluation process. Once Brian was diagnosed as having Attention-Deficit/Hyperactivity Disorder, we understood that he had a legitimate neurobiological condition and was not obstinate and uncooperative for the sake of being difficult. Dr. O— gave us complete yet understandable descriptions of the disorder and what to expect. I was developing great trust in her. She suggested medication in addition to her behavior modification program. We agreed; Brian's pediatrician once more prescribed methylphenidate. Brian took 5 mg with breakfast and another 2.5 mg with lunch.

During that time several reports circulated around the country that large numbers of children were being given this medication at the casual recommendation of teachers or parents. After reading and light research, I decided that, while this might be true in a few cases, most children being given the drug were under careful scrutiny by a doctor. Our child, at least, would be closely monitored.

Brian was now in his 12th week of kindergarten and was struggling. We explained his disorder to the teacher; she was most receptive to doing what she could to help. The doctors, with Mark and me, set up a schedule for Brian to take the medicine for a week, go off it for a week, then on again, for a month. We told his teacher that for the next month he would be medicated some days and not others. She would not know which days were which. This schedule was easy to "hide" from her; morning kindergarten meant he never needed to take a dosage while at school.

We spoke with the teacher every few days. At first there seemed to be no change; we were disappointed. In a few days, however, Brian was more cooperative, and she saw overall improvement. "It could be a coincidence. Don't jump to conclusions," we thought. But we hoped it was helping.

A week later, we had reports of some "bad" days. He seemed to be having problems again. "Still a coincidence?" we wondered, since he was now going to school without medication.

As the month progressed, the teacher's reports coincided closely with his medication schedule. We kept in touch through notes, telephone calls, and brief visits. She noted problems on the days Brian was unmedicated and had no comments or good reports on the days he had taken the medicine. We were becoming convinced that it was helping him.

When I picked him up after school one day during this trial period, his teacher met me with an exasperated look and said, but not unkindly, "He's off it, ain't he?" (He was.) Her mannerism and use of the word "ain't" were comical, though her message was not. I suppose I could have been offended but wasn't. She had been supportive and pleasant through this whole process.

During this month we took a trip to visit my brother 250 miles away. This trip was an ultimate test of the effects of the medicine. Mark and I became convinced that our lives and Brian's would be enhanced by his remaining on the medication. With boys aged 9, 5, and 1, a four-hour drive in a smallish car was something we always dreaded. The older boys wouldn't stay in their seatbelts. All three would wiggle and poke and fight most of the trip. I would be a wreck by the time we got there, since I sat in the back seat and refereed. On recent trips we had had to pull over, put the boys out on the roadside, and spank them or warn them to settle down. That was effective for 10 miles, if we were lucky. Unlike before, on this trip Brian (now on medication) noticed and talked about the passing scenery. He didn't resist (as usual) my attempts to sing songs together to pass the time. He read books and played with the travel games I always took along. In short, it was our first extended trip that was pleasant, relatively quiet, and nearly conflict free. This trip was too good to be true!

The three days spent at my brother's house were also great. There were the usual childish protests and the like, but this time was entirely different from what we were used to. Although she'd never said so, my sister-in-law had always had a hard time being around Brian. She tried to empathize, but I know he made her nervous. During that weekend she specifically told me that Brian seemed more grown up and that it had been a nice visit.

It was wonderful to hear for once how nice Brian had been!

This change had to be due to the medication. But we were still not totally comfortable giving it to him. It was almost scary that such a small dose could make such a difference. In meeting other parents of children with ADHD in the coming months, I learned that most did not respond to such a small dose. Yet many of them exhibit "night-and-day" differences with the aid of their medication. Mark and I agreed that using medication was the best thing to do. We began to see that if Brian were given the medication first thing in the morning, his ensuing behavior set the tone for the whole day.

Life was looking a bit more positive, or at least school was. In the beginning we did not give Brian medicine on evenings or weekends, because we wanted to keep the medicating to a minimum.

Weekends continued to be horrible, for the most part: Brian picked on his brothers. They fought back. Mark and I argued about how to discipline them. I started looking forward to Monday morning, when I could escape to my office. (I do enjoy my work, but this was going a bit too far.)

Finally, after further discussion with the doctors and seeing that Brian really did function better while medicated, we decided to give it to him on weekends also. Brian's actions and attitudes made it difficult for any of us to enjoy our time together. Our own adverse reactions to him were just as unpleasant. We could now see the advantage of continuity; he needed a constant reference point from which to develop his actions. Given that ADHD is a neurobiological disorder, it wasn't fair for Brian to have an aid one day and not the next.

This decision, like most, was not easy, and once again Mark was less convinced than I. But we agreed that Brian was more attentive and thus better behaved. The difference seemed remarkable. Not only was he happier, so were the rest of us. We finally felt like a "normal" family.

Other people also noticed a difference. Neighbors commented on his positive attitude, fellow churchgoers noticed his relative quietness, and my mother was relieved that Brian was no longer in constant turmoil. One fellow parishioner said to me, "He seems a lot quieter lately." Brian had recently started his weekend medication; I was pleased to know others saw a change. Rather than give the credit to the medication, however, I smiled at her and responded proudly, "He is growing up."

We had settled on a dosage of 5 mg in the morning and another 5 mg at noon. For the first 10 minutes, Brian tends to become quiet and sometimes withdrawn. Yet the positive effects are almost immediate. He can wake up "raring to go," be unwilling to get dressed, argue with his brothers over anything (or nothing), and cry that everyone is talking too loud. Within 10 minutes after taking his medicine, Brian can attend to his tasks. He can focus on getting ready for school and is willing to get ready without the earlier prodding. Some days he is even sweet to and tolerant of his little brother, Craig. The change still amazes me.

One Saturday morning when Brian was in second grade, all of us were awake early (a not uncommon occurrence). The boys were picking, fighting, poking, and tripping one another, as usual. Brad talked of meeting with a friend. Brian piped up that he and a boy, Jeff, had talked at school about playing together. I encouraged this rare happening, but Brian shrugged and now avoided the topic. Within 10 minutes of eating breakfast, which always included medication, Brian asked without any prompting, "Can I walk to Jeff's?" I was surprised and thrilled. "Nobody bother me. I want to get ready," he said. He dressed himself entirely, which also was rare, and off he went. Our jaws dropped in disbelief. Those actions and attitudes were so unlike Brian. The medication allowed him to focus on his intentions and follow through wonderfully. Alas, his friend was not home, but we praised Brian for his efforts and encouraged him to try again.

At age 8, Brian took 7.5 mg upon arising and 5 mg at lunch. We gave him another 5 mg later on days when we had school or social functions in the evenings. Subsequent increases over the years were in response to marked declines in his social or academic skills, increased aggression, and distractibility. He had started at a minimal dose, and increases were made in small increments, so they were not much concern for Mark and me.

Brian has always responded well to relatively low doses of methylphenidate. Since it is a short-lived medication, most children will exhibit a cycle of good performance during the peak time of medication and more difficulty when a dose is wearing off. We learned to time his activities and chores around his peak performance hours whenever possible.

Most children with ADHD return to inattentiveness and impulsivity after their medication has left their systems; evenings are a difficult time. Brian can also exhibit this pattern, but usually his good behavior during the day sets the stage for relatively calm evenings, which is, for us, an indirect or residual benefit of his taking the medication through the day. We have found that as Brian ages and becomes more in control of himself, lower rather than higher doses work well for him except for during school hours.

Some possible side effects of several medications given for attention deficits are insomnia, reduced appetite, and tics. Brian has displayed a throat-clearing tic, but it is sporadic and short-lived. His main side effect is a smaller appetite. He eats a decent breakfast but usually feels too full to eat much lunch. The evening meal brings varied responses; we serve him small portions, which he is expected to eat. (By insisting on a large meal, we would only be setting ourselves up for a needless battle.) By bedtime Brian is ravenous, because at that time the medicine has completely left his system. Our family always snacks before bed anyway, so we let him eat as much as he wants as long as one of the foods is healthy. For example, cookies are OK, but he has to have an apple, too. On most nights he would have a full bowl of cereal or two pieces of toast even after the cookies and apple.

As Brian got older, he remained thin but not unhealthy. By age 11, though, his weight had leveled off and he was so low on the charts that his doctor was concerned. So that summer we cut way back on his medication. His appetite rebounded, we fed him plenty of healthy food high in carbohydrates, and he had gained a few needed pounds by the time school began.

In past years medication was thought to be ineffective and no longer needed after puberty. But many adolescents and young adults struggled greatly after their medication was discontinued. Today we know that the neurobiological condition persists throughout the life-span. Therefore, adolescents and adults are now being effectively treated with medication.

Often adolescents resist taking their medication; they do not want to be thought of as different. They might not want to bother taking the few seconds to take a pill in the middle of the day, especially during school, when classmates may see them and question or tease them about it. Other adolescents or adults resist taking medication because it makes them seem weak or not in control of themselves.

One mother of an adolescent with ADHD told me that she and her son get into power struggles over whether or not he will take his medication on a particular day, even though he admits that it does benefit him. She has even noticed that when he has a special event going on or is especially wanting to impress someone (especially a female), he takes it readily on his own. It appears that he indirectly admits that the medication is, indeed, a positive influence in his life.

I can now say that Brian's medication is a lifesaver for him and the rest of us. It does not sedate him or calm him down in and of itself. Rather, it allows him to focus on what lies ahead and not be distracted and disturbed. It makes it easier for him to be tolerant of his brothers, to not feel the need to constantly trip, poke, and hit them. It helps Brian make the most of himself and to use his good qualities regularly. Brian's medication program has greatly improved his overall quality of life and thus that of our family as well.

Even on his "meds" he is not angelic by any means— I would not want him to be (although occasionally I wouldn't mind!). I certainly wouldn't want medication that "glazed" him over, that made him passive. Brian's medication greatly increases his attention span by enabling him to select what sound or activity to attend to. Secondary benefits are decreased distractibility and less sensitivity to noise. Because he is not overstimulated, he naturally acts less hyperactive.

Imagine yourself being constantly bombarded with noises—annoying, repetitive taps—and other people continually moving in and out of your sight. Anyone would become irritable and unpleasant. This is how life appears to the child with ADHD and makes him act as he does. This is what he needs to learn to screen out.

Our goal is to help Brian be an average boy with an average balance of good times and bad. For us, medication is part of the solution; yet it alone is only a part. Medical treatment will not cure the problem; ADHD does not simply go away. Our sessions in behavior modification, in understanding ADHD, and in learning to accept and cope with our feelings were essential to the whole process. It is the combination that has made our lives so much easier and fuller.

Modifying Behavior

A child's conduct can be greatly influenced by the presence of ADHD. Some of the common ADHD symptoms and possible resulting behaviors are:

Hyperactivity	Child is in constant, extreme motion, usually moving quickly and noisily, or is restless and fidgety
Distractibility	Child's attention is drawn to noises or motions in the room; he cannot complete a simple task
Impulsivity	Child does not consider consequences before he acts; impulsivity may lead to physical aggression

Nearly any adult can be taught about ADHD symptoms. He or she can read books, attend seminars, go through counseling, even obtain a degree in psychology. But all of that knowledge might be ineffective if that same adult faced daily living with a child with ADHD. Constant duress will usually overcome intelligent choices on how to manage a difficult child.

Most of the behaviors attributed to ADHD are not so much improper as they are terribly annoying and ever present. This disorder is insidious and pervasive. From rising in the morning to the last "goodnight," ADHD has the capacity to affect even the insignificant, everyday aspects of home life.

A child who is repeatedly acting in an inappropriate manner can leave the parent confused, frustrated, and possibly wondering at his own ineffectiveness in controlling his child.

A child with ADHD needs to be treated with structure and consistency, yet an already controlling or rigid parent must keep in mind that the child is not acting like he does on purpose. While structure is important, parents must not lose sight of the child's need for loving support.

If that same parent is headstrong or unsympathetic, his aggressive attempts at discipline can magnify the child's actions. Yet the child with ADHD could easily take advantage of and manipulate a permissive, submissive parent. Either way, neither parent nor child can break the cycle of ineffective interaction without help.

Mark and I fit somewhere between the above two examples. We are good parents, but after trying every method we knew to handle our frequent crises, we had still not come close to alleviating Brian's problems. We felt totally out of control of our own children, Brian in particular. We seemed to be in constant turmoil.

In his first 6 years, especially, Brian's emotional control was well below most children in his age group. I've read that a child with ADHD should be approached according to his emotional age, not his chronological age. I try to keep this in mind when I am disciplining Brian, but it is not easy to soften my approach when in the middle of family conflict.

Being a parent is a difficult job; parenting a child with special needs can be traumatic. Experts agree. "The ADD child is in a constant clash with [his] environment," said Barbara Ingersoll (1988) in *Your Hyperactive Child.* The authors of *Basic Handbook of Child Psychiatry* (Noshpitz, 1979) stated: "Their frustration threshold is reduced and outbursts of angry behavior are frequent. . . . for no apparent reason, the child strikes out blindly at all about him. Soon after being settled down, the child can be bewildered by what he has done and genuinely apologetic for it—only to undergo another uncontrollable crisis not long afterward" (p. 441).

"It is often hard to be sure whether you're having any effect . . . on a child with ADHD. Because of [the child's] poor impulse control . . . the disciplinarian may wonder whether there is any impact on the child at all," explained Friedman and Doyal, authors of *Attention Deficit Disorder and Hyperactivity* (1987).

Even after starting counseling, Mark and I had to work very hard at disciplining Brian in a way that was effective but not restrictive. Most parents will have to change their traditional methods of disciplining their child with ADHD. We found that Brian's baby-sitters, neighbors, and grandparents also needed to adapt their approaches to Brian to effectively interact with him. Awareness and change had to be a joint effort. Though my mother had a hard time accepting and understanding Brian's blatant improprieties, she was open to trying our methods.

After months (actually years) of calling attention to Brian's unacceptable behaviors, we had to deal with them constructively and try to approach him positively. Parents rarely compliment what they expect; instead, they punish the unexpected. It was not easy for Mark and me to replace our punitive, coercive, and often haphazard measures with a system of planned responses.

These planned, purposeful methods are referred to in counseling and treatment as behavior modification or behavior management. The terms *manage* and *modify* could be considered synonymous in dealing with Attention-Deficit/Hyperactivity Disorder. I feel that *modify* presents a gentler, more nurturing image than does *manage;* I'll therefore continue with modification in mind.

The goal of modifying the behavior of a child with ADHD is to change a behavior, not the feelings behind the actions. For example, it is normal and OK to be angry.

It might be normal for an angry child to want to hit his brother, but it is not OK to hit him. It is very hard for a child who is impulsive and aggressive not to hit someone, yet the presence of ADHD does not create an excuse for the child to get by with socially unacceptable actions. We needed to teach Brian which behaviors were socially improper and how to replace them with desirable ones.

Most of the suggestions we received through counseling, seminars, and books are a commonsense approach. The trick was to keep calm when faced with an emotional dilemma. I will admit we have often lost our wits and our tempers.

Ideally, any behavior modification plan will be implemented by a parent who is ever patient and consistent. That ideal cannot exist in real, everyday life. Each parent has his or her own personality, style of discipline, and strengths and weaknesses. But putting those weaknesses aside and sticking to these plans closely will surely bring progress and, probably, happiness for the parents and child alike.

The plans are outlined in many good books, some of which are listed in the References section on page 155. A professional dealing with children with special needs would also have helpful ideas and information. Going through the whole process takes time, commitment, and perseverance. Prayer also helps.

Nearly every suggested plan uses time-outs or rewards or both. Even after years of getting nowhere in effectively disciplining Brian, I resisted the idea of rewarding him. I was not comfortable with "bribing" my children to behave well. I had to admit that we needed to try something different, so we committed ourselves to do as Dr. O— suggested.

When Mark and I seriously used the suggested methods to modify Brian's behavior, we found out that they did indeed work. Also, Brian's medication now helped him to remember our requests and follow through with them. We began to work as a team instead of constantly battling one another.

Curbing Brian's physical aggressions was our first concern and the most challenging to modify. He also needed help with staying on task and becoming more cooperative and less oppositional.

Physical Aggression

Time-outs were a good solution to handling Brian's physical aggressions. He needed to be removed from the situation to cool down, and those around him were in no more danger of being hurt.

Brian frequently hit, kicked, poked, or otherwise assaulted others. These aggressions were not limited to his brothers; when very angry, Brian would strike at Mark, me, his grandmother, or anyone near him. When he acted this way, Mark or I would pick him up and put him in another room. For the most effective discipline, we should have remained calm, but we didn't always manage that!

Mark and I chose not to use Brian's bedroom for his time-outs. We want each of the boys to view his room as a pleasant place—a sanctuary, not a prison. I believe that is why we have had relatively little trouble getting any of them to go to bed at night.

The first-floor bathroom was our time-out room. It meant less hauling him up and down stairs, and we could continue our other activities with little time spent to check on him or set timers. It was also a boring place for Brian to be—no toys, no outside view, nothing to play with. (We did have cleaning supplies locked safely in another room.) At first he repeatedly flushed the toilet for something to do. Instead of yelling at him to stop, we added time to his "sentence," so he soon quit.

We needed to state what he had done wrong. For example, "Brian, you tripped your brother." Often, in his rage, he would not be aware of what he had actually done to hurt others.

One of the first times Brian was in time-out in the bathroom, he kept opening the door and shouting out, "Daddy, you were naughty" and "You were naughty again." He kept this up; when he quieted down, I allowed him to leave the room. I then saw that Brian had a red marker with him; he had made a series of hash marks on the wall, one for each time Daddy was "naughty"!

Our early attempts of "Stay here until you're ready to be good" were useless. He would come out and repeat his offense time and again. Even "Stay here for five minutes" did not work, because he would scream for the full time; when he rejoined us he was more agitated and aggressive than before. The whole scene would have to be repeated. So we settled on "Stay in here until you have been quiet for three minutes." After he had quieted, we would set a timer and notify Brian that the 3 minutes was beginning. When the buzzer sounded, he could rejoin us; we would thank him for quieting down and then drop the issue.

Lecturing him and dwelling on the bad feelings were not effective. He had little remorse and did not care if he had hurt others, physically or emotionally. All he could recognize was his own anger and confusion.

Time-outs longer than 5 minutes were rarely effective. By then, Brian would have forgotten why he was there and be distracted by and totally engrossed with a fly on the ceiling or a crack in the wall.

The first days we started the plan Brian would scream and storm around before settling down. He would blame his brother ("He started it") or his disciplinarian ("Dad, you're so mean") or deny his guilt ("I didn't do it"). It was very hard for me to listen to his rage and keep him separated in that room. No matter how annoyed I may have been at him to place him in time-out, upon hearing his cries I wanted to calm and protect him. I had to force myself to stick with it.

Within a week Brian settled down sooner. He learned there was a correlation between his calming and the overall length of the time-out. (Remember, it did not officially begin until he was quiet.) He was probably beginning to realize he was responsible for his actions.

Mark and I had been frustrated in the past that our disapproval, no matter how lovingly or how angrily we expressed it, had no effect on changing Brian's behavior. Most children will change their actions when others react unfavorably toward them. Like the typical child with ADHD, Brian could only change when his own time and space were being directly and methodically altered. We had to reinforce Brian's actions many, many times before a new habit replaced the old.

By the second or third week, Brian associated his behaviors with the consequences of time-out. Because he did not care to sit in the bathroom alone, be began to make an effort at curbing his aggressions. He was now developing a habit of proper behavior.

Brian's physical assaults, and therefore his time-outs, were becoming less frequent. Tension among all of us was ebbing. Brian was happier—he was not being yelled at all the time. His brothers were happier—they were not being hit or kicked so much. Mark and I were happier— we did not expend all our energies to keep peace among the boys.

We were two highly frustrated parents who were finally feeling a bit less pressured and worried. When Brian's aggressions subsided, so did the feelings they evoked in us. It was easier for Mark and me to be more patient with each other and the children. Thus, they would respond to us more readily and more cheerfully. Our family attitudes were changing—slowly but surely to be more positive than before we started the behavior modification plans.

Mark and I had to force ourselves to remain pleasant and patient. Only then were we able to discipline with a purpose rather than punish for the moment. Brian responded much better to this, which eased our tensions. In time, our former cycle of negativism began to reverse itself into an upward climb, as shown in Figure 8.1.

We still had a long, long way to go. A specific plan to curb Brian's aggressions was our first step. That step was, oh, so difficult. The rest did come easier. Once we could see that our earlier efforts proved fruitful, we had the desire to work on modifying other areas of concern.

Completing Tasks

Any household with children has the typical scene of Mom trying to get everyone to hustle out the door to school or to get the children to do their daily chores. We tried not to be always after the boys, saying "Do this, do that."

Charts for morning tasks helped Brian, but we still usually had to remind him to check the chart, as he would wander off or get distracted midway through his tasks. Figure 8.2 shows an example of a chart we used for him at age 5.

We learned to use simple commands for Brian. Instead of "Put on your shoes" every morning, the simple reminder of "shoes" was less threatening and more easily processed and remembered by Brian. I also found that just setting the shoes in front of Brian with no oral command was effective and did not make him feel pressured. These brief commands work well for the other boys, too; Mark and I still use them frequently.

Brian rarely completed even a simple job without several reminders. He could hardly pick up a pair of socks

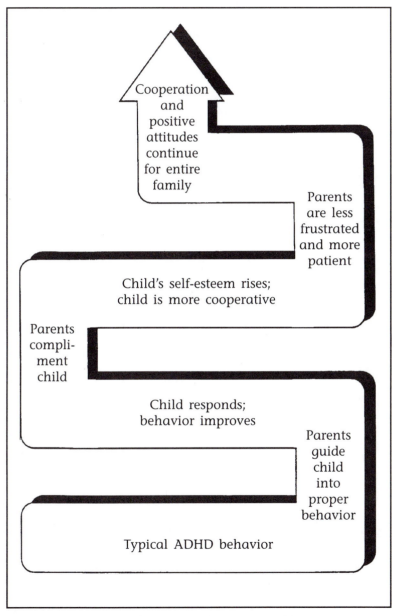

Figure 8.1. Upward-spiral effects of behavior modification techniques.

Figure 8.2. Example of Brian's chart for morning tasks.

and put them both on without being distracted or wandering off. This behavior might be typical for a 2- or 3-year-old, but having to keep him on task when he was 5 or 6 was a definite source of tension. We hated to always be badgering him, but it seemed the only way to get anything done.

It would seem simple to change the cycle of our yelling and Brian's not responding. But we were in a rut. Books and clinic information on behavior modification plans gave Mark and me a start. We learned to be creative with them and adapt them to suit Brian's needs and personality.

Once I understood that ADHD prevented him from completing tasks, I was more patient with him. The typical child with ADHD usually intends to do as he is asked. As he heads in the proper direction, he is easily diverted and forgets his original intention. Any sight, sound, or thought can distract the child enough to interfere with his actions. Though he is not trying to misbehave, he appears to be irresponsible, and his actions do not conform to others' expectations.

Brian is an exceptionally distractible youngster; he is keenly aware of his struggles to concentrate. I have learned to accept this distractibility; I try to help him through difficult situations and not feel stressed by them. Of all Brian's ADHD symptoms, distractibility is the easiest for me to cope with; it is less direct and defiant than the others.

Opposition and Noncompliance

His noncompliance was more difficult to contend with. Brian had developed a habit of outright denial of practically every request we made. He opposed most ideas and suggestions from us, whether they asked anything of him or not. Mark has commented that we could offer him ice cream and he would refuse it just to be difficult; this statement is not far from the truth.

Even when Brian complied with our requests, his frequent "side trips" and inadvertent actions on the way complicated his progress and frustrated the rest of us. This scenario was typical: On his way to find his shoes, he might stop to grab some crackers, half of which end up in crumbs on the floor. He gets to the porch and puts on one shoe. The neighbor's dog barks; Brian heads out the door to see the dog. I call Brian back; his shoelace gets caught in the door and he falls and cries. The other shoe can't be found. Craig calls for me, and in the time it takes for me to turn and ask, "What do you want?" Brian has slipped away and out of sight. He is not meaning to be rude; he just responds to what his mind is on. Even in the most innocent of actions, a child with ADHD can provoke irritation, anger, and frustration in others.

While acts of aggression put Brian promptly into time-out, we took a positive approach for modifying Brian's noncompliance: the reward system.

Rewards can be either tangible (candy, money, extra TV time) or intangible (a hug or praise). Mark and I were reluctant to give rewards, but they did work. It helped when we thought of them as reinforcements to our plan rather than as bribes. Taking away a privilege or favorite toy can also serve as reinforcement. We tended to stay with rewards, since they seemed more positive.

Our doctor and every book I read stressed that proper behavior must be promptly rewarded each time it occurs. I found this very tedious, but we charted Brian's progress by checking off on a progress chart each time he did what we had asked. Brian had to comply without complaining or reminders from us. Mark and I tried not to make too many requests. We also made sure that Brian had heard and understood what we wanted. We could then determine whether he wasn't comprehending our requests or was ignoring them.

I would often cup his chin in my hand so he could not turn his head. Even then, his eyes would wander. Then I would say, "Look at me" and repeat my directions when we had direct eye contact. It was also helpful to have Brian repeat the command back to me to be sure he had heard and understood. In time, I had only to touch his chin with my finger and he would respond by looking and listening.

Mark and I kept the progress chart prominently displayed on the refrigerator. At first Brian received an *X* and a small reward each time he showed cooperation and compliance. We gave him snacks as immediate rewards; some children like stickers or pennies. He took satisfaction in seeing his line of *X*s grow and in hearing our praise. At first he didn't catch on to the social reasons for complying or how they affected our overall family functioning. But the important thing was that he was becoming less oppositional and more cooperative. We saw improvement within the first week. Brian was learning to stop and think before he acted.

During the second week we began to taper the frequency of his rewards. Now Brian worked toward a daily goal. He still received an X each time he complied. That simple X, along with a hug or word of praise, was his immediate reinforcer. A predetermined number of Xs brought him a single, more enticing reward. At the end of each day we would see if he had earned, for example, an extra 15 minutes of playtime before bed. Mark and I were more comfortable with the plan once we were accumulating points rather than frequently giving small rewards.

Then tangible rewards dropped from daily to weekly. Mark and I found it satisfying to use rewards that were beneficial to the entire family. We gave end-of-the-week rewards, such as a canoe ride, a picnic, or a walk to the ice cream shop. Group activities helped teach Brian the social benefits of cooperative behavior. With our tension and stress level lower, we now enjoyed one another more. The family fun and unity also rewarded Mark and me for our efforts.

We also implemented charts for our oldest son. They helped teach Brad to control his temper and also made Brian feel less singled out. We also began them for our youngest son; Craig responded especially well to stickers as reinforcers.

Once established, there were times we needed to adapt our approach. Too much repetition eventually lost its effectiveness—also seen in the majority of children with ADHD. For a year or two I spoke clearly and briefly when making a request of Brian. He responded well. When he was 7, however, he decided I was babying him and resisted when I spoke that way. I had to consciously change my tone of voice and choice of words to elicit a positive response from him.

Children with ADHD need consistency but desire a great deal of variety. That seems contradictory, but consistency **and** variety can be implemented into a behavior modification plan. In fact, I have come to believe that the combination is crucial for success.

Mark and I have learned to be consistent while working to modify a single behavior. But Brian would quickly tire of the plan, and so it would lose its effectiveness. Once that behavior has been changed satisfactorily, a new method would be more effective for the next plan. For example, if we were using our picture chart with check marks for getting ready in the morning, we would switch to smiling or sad faces for the next behavior we wanted to modify. Brian would see this as new and interesting and would be more likely to respond. We took our plans step by step, one behavior at a time.

We were reminded in *Living with Children* (Patterson, 1976), "If a response isn't reinforced once in awhile, even after it is learned, [the response] is likely to weaken and perhaps disappear. . . . Positive reinforcers are necessary not only to teach a person new behaviors but also to maintain those he already has."

Mark and I do get lax; some days we simply give up. But then we always end up facing the same old annoyances. Brian cannot stay on track without our intervention and guidance. Helping a child with ADHD is a constant, ongoing process.

Discipline Versus Punishment

Most behavior modification techniques suggested for children with ADHD are the same as for effectively handling any child; the difference in the family coping with ADHD is that the techniques are required more often and more consistently. After much reading and professional counseling, Mark and I have found the following techniques especially helpful:

Be consistent. The child needs to know what to expect from you. I often accuse Mark of being too rigid, of never bending the rules. Though I know being consistent is ideal, it is one of the hardest things I've tried to do.

State your expectations clearly. "Clean your room" is not specific enough for a child. Instead, "Make your bed, pick all toys off the floor, and hang up your pajamas" tells him exactly what you expect. Better yet, write the separate tasks on a sheet of paper for the child. Do remember the child's maturational, not his chronological, age when assigning tasks. We had to learn to make our demands reasonable, considering Brian's limited abilities.

Break projects into small tasks that the child can remember and handle. By the time his bed is made (if he even finishes that), he will have forgotten the next command. Within 30 seconds of approaching the toys, he will be distracted enough to completely forget he should be picking them up instead of playing with them.

Give each direction one at a time. Let the child complete each task before you request the next one. Or write the tasks down so the child can check them off one by one, which will give him a feeling of accomplishment and success.

We often reminded Brian by asking "What are you supposed to be doing next?" which is less threatening than "Why aren't you picking up those toys?" It also taught him to think for himself and to stay on task.

Be explicit in your praise as well as your commands. "You had good manners at the table tonight" is too general. Give him something concrete to base his next day's behavior on: "You did a great job of sitting still in your chair and not playing with your food. We all had a pleasant meal."

Don't lecture. If you do, your child can then turn and put the blame on you. "You never told me that" and

"It's all your fault" were common reactions from Brian. Mark had a hard time not arguing with Brian or giving him long explanations. I learned to keep quiet; Brian knew the situation and tried to manipulate it in his favor.

Let the child learn the natural consequences of his negative behaviors. I often asked the boys to join me for a summer evening walk; Brian often refused to come with us. It seemed he was intent on being contrary, even when he knew we might stop for ice cream. If I pleaded or insisted, he would balk more. So I would take Brad and Craig; upon our return with cones in hand, he would scream because he didn't get any. Yet, true to the nature of his ADHD, such consequences did not have long-term effects; the next invitation to walk would likely produce the same scene. It took many years for Brian to connect actions with consequences and to adjust his behavior accordingly.

Give one warning and act swiftly on it. Carry through each time. Don't repeat or give second chances. As Dr. Tom Phelan in his *1-2-3 Magic* program (1990) urged, "Act, don't yak!" I often gave too many warnings to avoid bringing on conflict. I had to learn to insist on cooperation the first time, even though I struggled to follow through.

Pick your battles. A family living with ADHD is often already conflict ridden; do not add to it unnecessarily by badgering the child about every little thing. Choose the actions or attitudes that are truly important. Mark developed a rule that "matters of health and safety for self or others" were important, and we held firm on those issues. It was difficult not to be always after Brian about something, but we learned to ignore what was "merely" annoying and act on what was truly misbehaving.

Mark and I became proficient at brief commands. In fact, I grew to hate hearing the same things over and over. Two of our most famous quotes were "Keep your hands and feet to yourself" and "Not in my face." (Brian had a terribly annoying habit of sticking his hands in someone's face and wiggling his fingers.)

Brian, at times, could not be detained in one spot, even during time-out. He would relentlessly slide off the chair and run off, despite warnings, pleading, yelling, or spanking. No punitive measures seemed to matter to him. Once I put Brian back into time-out nine times for the same offense. He still did not calm down or stay there. Ideally I should have kept it up until he finally listened to me. Usually I gave up long before nine times; my patience wore thin and my anger mounted. Many times I turned my back on him and walked away, though I knew I should carry through. I was so frustrated and angry I had to leave the situation for his own safety. Nothing short of physical restraint would have made him stay put.

Brian's psychologist suggested locking him in his room until he settled down. If done, the "lock-in" should be supervised; a parent should remain on the other side of the door. Though I know Brian would have settled down quicker when isolated, I could not bring myself to do that.

"The frustration of raising a child with ADHD makes parents vulnerable to the use of physical punishment" (p. 63) warned authors Friedman and Doyal (1992). I admit Mark and I have at times been too harsh. A persistently oppositional child is definitely at risk for abuse. Without our strong family backgrounds and mutual efforts to work out our problems, Mark and I might easily have resorted to the same thing. It is scary to realize and admit this, but the emotions evoked from dealing with a child like this can be overwhelming.

Mark and I tried to be aware of when the other was at the breaking point and step in to let the other "escape." My best way of calming down was to go for a walk around the block. It is important for every parent to discover his or her own nondestructive way of coping and becoming calm.

Brian always has responded much more strongly to Mark's discipline than to my own. Mark could do as little as speak Brian's name firmly, and Brian would run off wildly, screaming, "Save me from this madman." That was Brian's theatrical way of drawing attention away from his misbehavior and putting the blame on Dad. Another way Brian expressed his resistance was to call his dad "King of the World." Needless to say, Brian was not on bended knee! Brian also tried to manipulate me into feeling sorry for him. It usually worked, though I got pretty good at not letting my feelings interfere with our disciplinary measures.

Parents need to spot and avoid difficult situations before they happen. I am instinctively alert to Brian's level of activity for the day. I can anticipate problems and reroute Brian into a different activity before real problems occur. Prevention is much more pleasant, and actually easier, than punishing after the event. Mark and I were more effective and happier when we used our energies positively and preventively.

Even now, if I hear the boys getting irritated with one another during a game, I step in and try to dissuade them. Something like "Hi guys" or "You've been playing nicely" reminds them to interact positively and sets them back on the right track. We cannot avoid all conflict; they must learn to settle their own differences. If I catch them before the conflict is intense, they will sometimes work it out on their own.

Attention-Deficit/Hyperactivity Disorder is not a visible handicap, but it is very real. As *CH.A.D.D. Educator's Manual* (Fowler, 1992) has pointed out, "These children behave in a way that comes naturally to them" (p. 8). A child shouldn't be punished for something he cannot help.

We've adjusted our expectations to fit Brian's abilities. It was not fair, even when he was 8, for us to expect him to sit still and "proper" in a restaurant. And he cannot yet in middle school finish an hour of homework all in one sitting.

We now avoid situations that will obviously lead to disaster. Mark and I plan activities at times of the day that seem best for our children. When we go out to eat, it is at a family-style restaurant, and even then we arrive early. That way we beat the crowds so as to disturb fewer people, and we get served faster, which means less time for the boys to get impatient and disruptive. We do have rules of conduct during these times, however; one cannot toss out rules and use this disorder as an excuse.

Group activities are stressful for Brian, and we do not always participate in them. If Brian is having a particularly difficult day, Mark and I either cancel the event for that evening, get a sitter for Brian, or one of us stays home. To not go is not always fair to the rest of us, but it would be less fair to go and have it be a disaster.

It is natural for Mark and me to give our children praise and plenty of hugs and kisses. Yet it was difficult to look cheerfully on Brian when he created so much tension in our family. Mark and I had to break our pattern of using blame and criticism to regulate Brian's behavior. I knew we were devastating his already fragile self-esteem, but we could not seem to break the cycle without outside help.

In one of our parents' groups for those with children with ADHD, we discussed our children's low self-esteems. Many parents found it difficult to speak positively about their children. We parents agreed that when given a sincere compliment, most of the children reacted in one of two ways. Some children would "milk" the parent for all the attention they could get. They needed to be continually pumped up with compliments or favors to feel good about themselves. Brian had this reaction; his need for attention and compliments was insatiable. Others would shrug off the compliments or deny their good qualities. Dr. O— said it best during one of our counseling sessions: "It is as if they have nothing inside to hang a compliment on."

Rather than criticize Brian personally, Mark and I had to learn to make him aware of his actions and how they needed to change. We strove to pick out what good qualities we could and comment on them. "You did a good job of cooperating when getting dressed" was difficult when he was already bounding down the hall intent on bugging his brothers. But positive comments eventually accumulated in Brian's mind and made a difference. They also reminded Mark and me, in our frustration, that this child could be lovable.

I've always appreciated Brian's loving nature and his quick mind and desire to learn. Once we were all under better control and had lightened up, we discovered a wit about him as well.

My maternal instinct was to protect my child from all the confusion and frustration he struggled with. I knew his problems were just as hard on Brian as they were on the rest of us; he was the one who felt all "scribbly." With Dr. O—'s help, Mark and I learned to look at the disorder as being the problem rather than Brian being the problem. Now we saw our goal was to overcome ADHD, not to overcome our child. We allied ourselves with Brian against his difficulties.

Together, we're making a difference.

Emotions

9.

The "terrible twos" is usually a difficult time for children and their parents; it is an age of extreme emotions. Brian ran well beyond the twos with his emotions out of control. Even before knowing about ADHD, I often wryly described Brian as "age five going on two." It was like living with the *same* 2-year-old for 3 years in a row. Brian did very little emotional maturing during that time.

I have read that living with a child with ADHD is like living on an "emotional roller coaster." It is safe to assume that being a child with ADHD is like being on that same ride—unceasingly.

On the positive side, Brian also has strong endearing emotional qualities: he can be caring, affectionate, and sensitive. I call him my "sweetie boy" because he is just that. Brian loved to hug and at 8 years old still wanted a goodnight kiss. I was glad to comply, but there, too, he got carried away. He'd hug so hard and long that it was uncomfortable and annoying for Mark or me. Brian wouldn't let go at our request; sometimes we needed to pry him away. Brian, like most children with ADHD, is unpredictable in his responses. While at times he would balk at our touch, other times he could not get enough of it. There is no way to anticipate what his reaction will be at any given time, but whatever the reaction, it is likely to be intensely expressed.

"The ADHD child is insatiable . . . enough is never obtained," Dr. Dale Jordan (1992) stated. We seem to never let Brian eat enough, play long enough, talk to him enough, or travel far enough to suit him.

We probably do more activities (golf, canoe, bowl, picnic) as a family than most. Yet Brian feels he never has any fun. Dr. Jordan continued, "The[ir] emotional needs can be a bottomless pit that cannot be filled. No matter how much love and affection ... it is never enough. The child whines and badgers and pleads for more."

We could spend all day in an amusement park— riding, sliding, eating—and on the ride home Brian would still complain it wasn't enough. Two days later he would whine, "When are we going to do something fun?" These kinds of responses exasperate Mark and me, and often anger us.

Brian's psychologist feels that these difficulties were related to his low self-esteem. Though emotionalism is not a symptom of ADHD, the presence of ADHD puts a child at risk for being highly emotional.

Many actions that adults view as negative or unacceptable are "the child's way of trying to express ... other emotions, while on the surface he shows only the irritating and provocative behavior." This excerpt from *Your Hyperactive Child* (Ingersoll, 1988) demonstrated how the child's low self-esteem often determines his attitudes and actions.

On the weekend of Brian's 8th birthday we spent 3 days camping, swimming, fishing, and canoeing. On our way home I asked Brian if he had had fun. My question was a set-up, since he almost never admits it even if he does enjoy himself. This time he simply smiled and said yes. What a welcome surprise after years of so much complaining!

A child or young adult with ADHD will almost always be less mature than his peers. Emotional outbursts are frequent because life seems harder for them. Even as a toddler, Brian viewed life more seriously and less playfully than the average child. "All the troubles in my life," he frequently sighed. "I wish I were dead" was his ultimate expression of despair and one that scared and deeply saddened me. We all lived day after day enveloped in the shadow of his struggles.

While he was 3 to 6 years old, Brian did a lot of crying. There were days when I seemed to do nothing but wipe his nose, settle him down, only to start all over again—cry, wipe, cry, wipe! He never had many true temper tantrums (in anger), but sad, emotional outbursts were common. He would throw up his arms, fall to the floor, and open his mouth wide and wail. This action became the one that irritated and angered me the most.

I adopted the "football" hold: to grasp him around his middle and carry him under one arm like a receiver carries the ball. I still use it on our third son, as I've found it a simple and effective way of carrying any child. He could then kick and flail his arms and legs without hurting himself or me. Holding Brian in the usual upright manner made him hard to hang on to. He was able to throw back his head and bang into a wall or doorway, a not uncommon occurrence. Then screams and tears of true pain would be heard as well, and more nose wiping and calming down had to be done.

By the time he was 7, going on 8, I no longer thought of Brian as tearful. Yet a new neighbor who was trying to keep straight which of the three boys was which, caught me by surprise when she asked, "Which is the one that cries a lot?" I realized he was still more tearful than other children his age.

Some mornings I tried to keep track of how many outbursts or conflicts required my intervention. At times they occurred every 5 minutes; that is 12 times in an hour! The first hour or two upon arising were the hardest; then the pace would slacken. Still, Brad and Brian would clash several times each hour, all day long. Mark or I would have to stop what we were doing, break them up, maybe call a time-out, and hope the peace would last. It usually didn't.

Brian seemed to need to readjust himself each day to interacting with the family and living with our rules. I grew to hate mornings. I could not leave Brad and Brian together long enough to shower or eat breakfast or even use the bathroom. They would instantly start fighting. After many frenzied mornings of getting ready for work and school while trying to handle the conflicts, I started taking one of them in the room with me, or at least to a different level of the house. This approach was preventive rather than punitive and worked better, but after a couple of minutes my "captive" would escape and seek out his brother. I got into a habit of yelling and spanking to make them stay put. Even then, they didn't comply for long.

Looking back, it seems silly that it took me years to put locks on the doors. I have joked that most people lock their bathroom doors to keep their kids out; I lock my doors to keep my kids in! But family peace is worth the price of privacy. I could then lock one of them in with me and get ready without interruption, which made a huge difference in my outlook on mornings; my mood, of course, affected the whole family in a good way. My goal was to keep the conflicts between Brian and his brothers at a minimum. Otherwise the negativism would escalate until we were all in bad moods.

I wrote in Brian's baby book when he was 3½ and again when he was 4: "Often uncooperative, whiny, and unsociable. Exasperating at times." I now feel bad that I was compelled to record those words in what is usually a diary of the child's progress and accomplishments, but at that point in time, that is all there was!

In a parents' group another mother told us that living with her son was like living with Jekyll and Hyde. She never knew when she spoke to him whether he would react lovingly or angrily. This same range of emotions made it difficult for us to maintain consistency with Brian. On some days Brian might be so wrapped up in his own difficulties that he would wildly refuse to comply with our requests, even though Mark and I remained calm and consistent.

It is very difficult to keep a child's self-esteem high when he is struggling with ADHD. Drs. Friedman and Doyal stated in their book *Attention Deficit Disorder and Hyperactivity* (1987) that the child with ADHD "is criticized more than other children [and] disaster seems to follow him. . . . Constant criticizing and punishment seem to confirm for the child that he is bad or stupid. He will handle that feeling by becoming obstinate, negative [complaining] and/or bossy." Other children might, instead, withdraw.

Positive reinforcement helps considerably. I wrote of Brian, then age 4½: "Behavior beginning to improve with lots of patience and positive reinforcement from Mom and Dad." Mark and I continued using praise and affection to counteract all the bad things that happened so often to Brian.

It is hard to find ways to compliment a child who is often whiny, uncooperative, and annoying. After months of seemingly constant criticism, it's no wonder a difficult child feels bad about himself. It's a tough situation—so many of Brian's actions were improper and needed to be reprimanded, yet we wanted not to be constantly "after" him. Consciously watching for little things to comment on was a start. Something simple like "Thank you for the hug" goes a long way in making any child feel important, loved, and more secure.

We made sure to notice when Brian did something *good* instead of something *bad*. "You did a good job of ignoring your brother's teasing" or "Thank you for being quiet in church" would reinforce what we'd been teaching him all along. But even such simple compliments sometimes were forced on our part when we were feeling overwhelmed by his misbehavior. Once we started, it became easier and more natural. Slowly but surely, each family member became more positive, more relaxed, and kinder to one another; we continued our upward spiral.

Brian still overreacts even to constructive suggestions and does not seem to value or learn from them. It's no wonder, after all those years of genuine criticism. Like the typical child with ADHD, Brian is outwardly defensive and storms at anyone when he feels threatened, whether that person meant to be critical or not.

Brad, while 8 to 9 years old, took the brunt of Brian's actions during what I call the "awful years"—just before diagnosis and counseling. Whenever he could, Brian poked, tripped, or teased Brad. Sometimes Brian struck out, physically or verbally, at Brad for a mere action or sound he was making that distracted and upset Brian. It is important to understand that most of Brian's actions were due to the nature of ADHD, which made it difficult for him to control his actions.

Brad would naturally retaliate; they would end up shouting, wrestling, and kicking. Most conflicts were initiated by Brian; however, we tried not to always blame him; it always takes two to tango (or in this case, to tangle). I cannot imagine how many times Mark and I have said, "I know you're angry, but that is no excuse to hurt another person." But their physical aggression did not cease. All they could think of (Brian especially) was their desire to react and strike out.

These actions and reactions are typical of any sibling relationship, but again the difference is that, because of ADHD, they were more constant and more forceful. A friend once described another child with ADHD whom she was familiar with by saying, "He is so intense." Medication and counseling have helped to lower the intensity of Brian's emotions and have brought his actions to a more normal level.

Progress in physical and social development naturally brought progress in the emotional sense. Once Mark and I worked on the behavior modification plans suggested by Brian's psychologist and did not need to discipline him so often, Brian brightened up so much. His sense of humor and clever way of saying things began to shine through. (Or was it that we were relaxed enough to hear and appreciate those qualities?) It was probably a combination.

But in the years before we learned of ADHD and how to help Brian, his interactions with his brothers as well as with Mark and me were conflict ridden. Add this to all the other issues to deal with, and an ADHD family sits upon a volcano of emotions, ready to sputter and erupt at any time.

Learning and the School Environment

10.

Brian learns easily and eagerly. When he was just 28 months, I noted in his baby book that he "learns fast and almost without Mom and Dad aware." Like most children, Brian learns best when covering a topic that he is especially interested in. He has always spent hours at a time, preferably by himself, at certain activities. From age 2 he has loved to play with a deck of cards, sifting through them or sorting them into piles of separate suits or numbers. At 28 months, he could properly identify each card.

When Brian was 4, he spent hours playing with cards alone. He invented scores of games, usually in some way categorizing the cards or toys or books on hand. Before he was 6 years old, his favorite activity was playing Monopoly. More often than not, he played alone, inventing and playing for an imaginary partner. Even years later I would hardly recognize his room without the board and money and hotels spread out on the floor!

Though Brian is *capable* of learning, his distractibility makes it *difficult* for him to listen and concentrate on what is going on. Children and adults with ADHD are poor listeners. Since listening is a key ingredient in learning, poor listening skills often hamper their learning. Dr. Russell Barkley has said that youngsters who have attention deficits might retain as little as 30 to 50% of oral messages they receive.

Attention-Deficit/Hyperactivity Disorder contributes to schoolchildren's forgetting assignments, losing papers, or handing in sloppy work. They may even neglect handing it in at all, even if finished. Getting a child with ADHD through school requires constant communication between parents, teachers, and other school personnel. Weekly progress reports are helpful. Daily notes between school and home may be necessary for highly unorganized students. The child should not be expected to be able to do well on his own. Drs. Friedman and Doyal (1992) warned: "It is natural . . . to [wonder] when he will learn to do his schoolwork by himself. . . . Keep forever in mind . . . that the child's inability to follow through, to stay organized, and get things done by himself . . . is a handicap that may require the . . . help of teachers and parents throughout [his] school career" (p. 99).

According to Goldstein and Goldstein (1989), there are two common times of referral for professional diagnosis of ADHD: the first organized school year (kindergarten or first grade) and in middle or junior high school, when demands increase and organization is a must.

For many children with ADHD, fine motor coordination is unpredictable and often inconsistent daily. Variability of performance is itself a characteristic of ADHD. The child might tie his shoes successfully one morning and have great difficulty the next. It is hard for a parent to know when to insist on results. For example, Mark might say, "Brian, put your shoes on." Even at 7 and 8 years old, Brian sometimes fumbled with getting them on his feet and had great difficulty tying the shoelaces. Since his frustration tolerance was low, he got discouraged and quit readily. Should Mark press the issue and insist that Brian do it himself? After all, he generally did it alone. Or could his dad help Brian this time without having him expect this help every day?

Before Mark and I were aware of Attention-Deficit/ Hyperactivity Disorder, we were often frustrated and angered over Brian's seeming unwillingness to complete chores that we knew he was capable of doing. He gave up so easily when his first attempts failed. We eventually realized that on any given day he needed much more time and guidance than he might have previously.

In school a child with ADHD might score 90% on a math test but do poorly on the same test on another day. He truly cannot recall the skills he used on the first test. The student is blamed for being lazy or for not really trying: "You could do it last week, why not today?" And the student does not know, for despite his efforts his knowledge and skills were unavailable during that second test. Inconsistencies such as these are an inherent part of the disorder.

In the school setting, children learn social concepts as well as academic ones. Socializing is difficult for many children with ADHD. Because of his impulsivity, a child will create tension within the classroom. He might wiggle and squirm in his seat, thus making the teacher nervous. His pushing and shoving in the hallway will anger other students. It is not uncommon for a child with ADHD to blurt out in class. For example, once Brian was so preoccupied by an itch he had that, after the teacher had ignored his raised hand, he stood up and announced his discomfort out loud.

The playground presents potential problems for any school-age child. A child with ADHD will experience more conflicts than most, especially if he is overtly hyperactive.

Schoolwork for most children with ADHD is a struggle. Written work is usually not neat, often because the child is in a hurry. Difficulty with fine motor skills further complicates the handwriting process. The child may have visual-motor deficiencies, which basically mean that what the child sees in his book or on the chalkboard is either forgotten or "jumbled" by the time his hand begins to copy it. Because ADHD is a group of symptoms caused by defective neurotransmitter processes, even high intelligence may not be available for organized use.

Labeling these children as lazy, messy, or immature will contribute to low self-esteem. Even if the child does not hear the words, others' attitudes toward him will convey the message. The child will either withdraw and become apathetic toward school or try to raise his self-esteem in other "acting-out" ways. One possibility would be to try to make himself feel better by rebelling: skipping classes, breaking rules, smoking, or vandalizing. He then gets into more trouble, confirms others' opinions of him, and is locked into a vicious cycle. The untreated student is at risk for becoming a high school dropout or being put into an alternative educational setting.

Many children with ADHD also have specific learning disabilities and require extra help to overcome them. Any child struggling in school should be tested for possible placement in special learning disability (LD) classes. A child already in an LD class should be completely assessed; ADHD or other disorders can disguise themselves as a basic learning disability and vice versa. Hearing or visual problems can also create similar difficulties; the child should be thoroughly tested for these as well. A complete and professional battery of tests should be run to determine the child's specific areas of need.

Fortunately, Brian exhibits no specific learning disabilities. He has a quick mind and a fine long-term memory, especially for numbers, facts, and detailed information. He seems to have tunnel vision that lets him tune in to certain activities. Ironically, it's simple directions and everyday procedures that Brian cannot seem to remember and follow through on.

Unlike many children with ADHD, Brian is a good reader. This ability will certainly help him through school. Yet it is hard to know how much he comprehends or retains; he's usually unwilling to discuss his readings or share information or ideas with us. He doesn't always get the whole concept of what the book is about, but certain details (e.g., names and numbers) stick out clearly in his memory—often those things easily passed by or forgotten by other children. It is common that these details that intrigue the ADHD mind are often not the main points on which teachers will test.

Even in a controlled environment, the child with ADHD might become engrossed with and distracted by nearly anything. The texture of the wall or even internal distractions like his stomach rumbling can cause him to forget what he was supposed to be working on. If left undirected, the hyperactive student would be wiggling and thinking a dozen different thoughts. The mind of a child with ADD (without hyperactivity) would be wandering aimlessly. The teacher must check in frequently and keep these children on task.

Helping with homework is something that most parents dread, and with children with ADHD, it can be a nightmare. Their lack of concentration and organization makes homework a real trial for the student and parents or other helper. Brian's writing skills are not great, and he is so distractible that on some evenings it takes much time, patience, and guidance to get him to complete even a half-page of work. Often we end early in frustration or anger at one another or at the situation.

Most children with ADHD perform well when approached on a one-to-one basis. Even if nothing is said, the physical presence of someone else helps Brian to keep his attention focused. When Brian is working on a math paper, for example, and doing the problems without hesitating, it is best for one of us just to be there and say nothing. Occasionally a simple "good" or smile will encourage him. By saying more or asking questions, he can get thrown way off track. Our quiet presence is a reminder for him to continue. Then if his eyes start to wander or someone else enters the room, we need to call him back to his work.

If we interrupt, no matter how good the intentions, Brian could be distracted enough to throw up his hands and complain, "You mixed me all up." By the time he calms down, picks up his pencil, and gets a new start, many minutes have been wasted.

His kindergarten teacher was quickly aware that Brian resists structured activities; yet this is how he performs best when in a group (with Brian, two or more people, including himself, is a group). By mid-year the teacher reported that Brian "shows steady progress with structured activities but has a difficult time making decisions during free time."

Parents must learn to offer structure in a manner that the child does not feel pressured or threatened. Yet organization must come initially from a parent or teacher. Structure is one of those things that children with ADHD need the most but like the least. In the classroom, conforming to a specific format can be difficult for these children.

On a one-to-one basis, an adult can enable a child with ADHD to focus his thoughts. In a large group or classroom situation, the child's mind drifts and he loses continuity of what is being said. The child does best with constant eye contact and occasional requests to repeat the direction, plus close physical presence to be sure he is paying attention. Again, these are difficult (though not impossible) to do in a classroom.

Brian became more attentive toward the end of his kindergarten year, mostly because of his medication. His teacher said that he still "has a slight problem focusing on a given task when the noise level is high." When she saw this happening, she moved him to a quieter part of the room.

Lack of organizational skills often hampers the child's learning. Dr. Harvey Parker, in *ADD Hyperactivity Workbook* (1988), has advised: "Because the child's perceptual system is lacking . . . the child may need to 'borrow' from the teacher's ability to organize" (p. 107). A distractible child can be helped by being seated near the teacher and away from distractions such as windows or talkative classmates; the fewer people in his field of vision, the fewer distractions he will have. Brian became so accustomed to being placed on the end of a row or in the front of the room that he still naturally chooses these spots when entering a room, regardless of the activity or purpose.

Brian is great at keying in on certain activities and pursuing them with vigor. He loves lists of almost anything: zip codes, ball game scores, and statistics of any kind. I constantly find sheets of paper containing columns of numbers from one activity or another. Figure 10.1 is an example of one he did at age 7; he had invented a game with marbles and kept score according to their colors.

Brian's other passion is maps. As a second grader, he knew more about geography than many high school students. He has read a book about the 50 states countless times, as well as a child's world atlas. Brian readily memorizes the names of cities and rivers, the colors and designs of national flags, and the like.

One day when Brian was 7, I surprised him with a wall-size world map. He could already identify nearly all the states plus many countries. The new map increased his interest and therefore heightened his skills. I dubbed him our "Map Whiz."

The summer he turned 8, Brian took a short class in stamp collecting. Sorting and putting the stamps into categories and columns was just his thing. When I visited his classroom I saw that he was also keeping a running

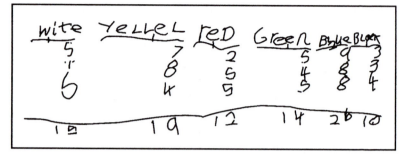

Figure 10.1. Brian's invented game using lists.

total of the stamps' face value. As he pasted each one in place, he would add its amount to his current total. I was not surprised—this was so like him. Such unique qualities make him as delightful as he can be difficult.

There is a danger that the child with ADHD may be automatically pegged a "poor student" or "low achiever." Early in our searching years, I found myself tending to do that to Brian, maybe in part to avoid later disappointment for all of us. Many of these children are thought of as lazy, immature, or irresponsible. There is no question that they have a higher than average chance of social and scholastic difficulties or even failure. But I firmly believe that with careful guidance and effort each individual can be taught to achieve his full potential.

We used a "goal card" system for Brian throughout elementary school. It served three purposes: to monitor Brian's performance at school, to provide him with a reinforcement system, and to facilitate communication between home and school. We used a simple but effective system, adapted from Harvey Parker's *ADD Hyperactivity Workbook* (1988) (see Figure 10.2).

It took the teacher less than 30 seconds to fill it out each day. We signed the card each night so the teacher knew we were aware of what kind of day Brian had had. We tried to choose one behavior that he would be successful at and two that he needed to work on. It was set

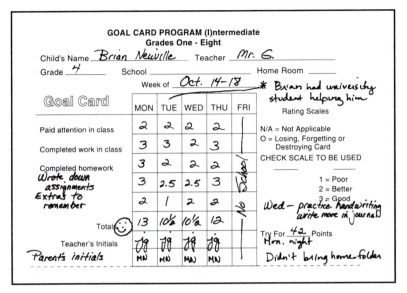

Figure 10.2. Example of Brian's goal card.

up so that he would reach his goal more often than not. It was crucial for us to periodically change the target behaviors and the rewards to keep the system interesting and challenging for Brian—an example of providing variety within structure.

For young children, stickers could be used in place of the numbers. Rewards for reaching the week's goal can be adapted for each child: extra TV time, candy, a walk to the park, or whatever that child will be motivated to work for.

I told Dr. O— when Brian was about 10 that I hoped to get him through school with little more difficulty than if he had no disorder at all. She warned that this may not be realistic. It has, indeed, taken continued efforts; for me, the process has been as emotionally wearing as it has been physically tiring.

I try to refrain from making too many special requests of teachers at the risk of seeming demanding or overprotective. Yet if I ever feel that Brian is disturbed or floundering because he needs more guidance, I will always make his needs known to the teacher and be sure someone follows through with my requests. I've been fortunate that in our schools we've rarely had to be forceful. If a teacher is reluctant to try what I've suggested, I will ask if it can be tried for just 2 weeks and then we'll talk again and see how it is going. It's hard for someone to say no to that request, and inevitably, Brian was doing better and the teacher's job had become easier as well.

For parents dealing with an uncooperative school system, I strongly urge them to keep trying. Provide your child's school with accurate, up-to-date information on the disorder and highlight the areas that your child has particular difficulty with. Also, let your child's teacher know of his talents and assets. Throughout elementary and into middle school, Brian worked with the school's speech pathologist. He also received a year of occupational therapy, which strengthened and improved his fine motor skills. I made sure the guidance counselors kept track of Brian's performance as well; they proved to be good advocates when we needed them.

As stated in a United States Department of Education's 1991 Policy Memorandum, all U.S. public schools are obligated to provide services to students with ADHD who are shown to be in need of instructional adaptations. Most of the things that are good for students with ADHD—written instructions to supplement verbal ones, repetition of important facts, and the like—are good for *all* students. It's just that the students with ADHD *need* these aids to succeed.

Teachers should be informed by the parents that they are sincerely trying to make the teachers' jobs easier as well as benefit their own children. Above all, teachers must understand that the child's inattentiveness and idiosyncrasies are *not* intentional. To help the teacher act on his or her new awareness, a parent can offer assistance in any way possible and ask for periodic feedback from the child's teachers. If it does not come (teachers are busy), a call or visit to the school to get the information will be necessary.

So often the students with ADHD are truly trying their best, but that "best" is usually not good enough. They have encountered so many obstacles and failures that most of them see the world in black and white; when part of an assignment is done wrong, they feel they did it all wrong. Most teachers will be positive and encouraging if they are aware of a child's low self-image.

A student with ADHD must have outside help with most assignments. Study partners or tutors can be helpful, especially for the student in middle or high school or college. Tape-recording lectures can free the student's mind to concentrate on listening rather than trying to take notes. Many, including Brian, produce more work of better quality by doing assignments on a word processor rather than relying on their poor handwriting skills.

Once students reach middle and high school, they have no single teacher who looks after all their needs. A homeroom teacher or guidance counselor would be a good person to advocate for a teenager and act as a liaison between the teachers and the parents. Teachers at this level are trained to encourage children to be independent and self-sufficient. Teachers who are reluctant to offer children extra help may say they want to prepare them for "the real world." The adolescent with ADHD must prepare for that as well but will need more time and more guidance than his peers who are not disordered. Students can be taught an organized system of keeping track of assignments. We check up on Brian's assignments nightly, often to his dismay! We do not do his homework for him but make sure that he has completed what he should and that it's in his folder for the next day.

Another aspect of educating children with attention deficits is involved for those who do well academically.

They need to be challenged in those areas to keep them from feeling bored. Boredom could lead to a wandering mind and even more restlessness than usual. Those children with hyperactivity may be requiring so much effort to curb certain behaviors that any potential for giftedness is overlooked. Brian's fifth-grade teacher recognized his talent in math and allowed him to work ahead of the rest of the class. Brian felt proud of himself and worked hard without prodding to complete his work. He completed the fifth-grade book and some of the sixth, working independently under the supervision of his teacher, and received all A's.

The following year Brian was placed in an accelerated math course. Ironically, he did not fare so well in that, largely because he did not complete assignments or score well on the formal tests. Brian did exceptionally well with facts and concrete ideas but not so well with abstract concepts or sequential activities. He had little problem with comprehension, but his lack of production brought him down. These occurrences are common for students with ADHD. Brian ended that math class with quarter grades of: B, A-, D, and B. Again, this high variability in performance is typical of students with attention-deficit disorders.

Many individuals with ADHD can actually concentrate for long periods on something that highly interests them. This hypervigilance is clearly shown in Figure 10.3, an example of work that Brian did in sixth-grade math class. The class was given a division problem; Brian was intrigued that the answer had a remainder and became determined to find an answer without a remainder. So he kept dividing and dividing, adding place points, and taping on extra sheets and strips of paper as was needed! I don't think that he finished any more of that night's assignment, but he could be seen for days working on the same problem that held him captive!

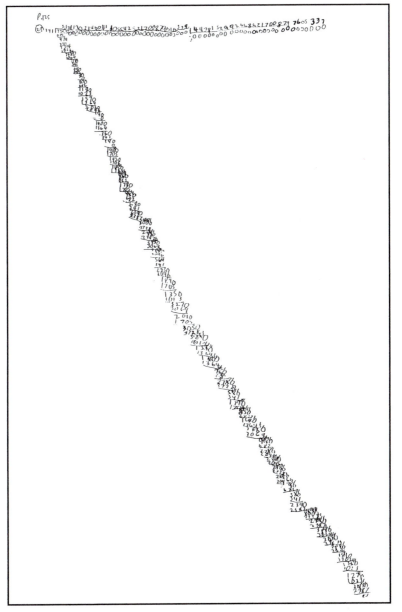

Figure 10.3. Brian's math division problem.

I hope that some day Brian will be able to guide his intense interests into a talent that will enable him to gain and hold a good job.

Brian is developing some fine characteristics that I truly never thought I would see in him. He is doing better all the time and is learning his own way, whether his grades always reflect it or not. But it is amazing how he still loses assignments and forgets notes and all those seemingly simple tasks that even older students with ADHD seem to struggle with. Yet I am confident that Brian will continue to progress, with the help of Mark and me and the medical and educational professionals with whom we've teamed up.

I'm not as confident that Mark and I will have the patience or fortitude to direct Brian always as we should. I'm sure there will be many more evenings of tears and resentment; Brian resists the very structuring he needs so much. It will take awareness, effort, and patience on everyone's part for him to succeed.

Social Skills

There are many ironies in the behaviors of those individuals afflicted with Attention-Deficit/Hyperactivity Disorder. Even while oblivious to others' reactions to him, Brian was often perturbed at similar actions by others. When children tease Brian, he's easily hurt and angered. Yet, if he does the teasing, he doesn't understand why they take offense. I saved a note from him, written during second grade, that says, "I hate my group in math they are so mean, fast, rude and loud and dumb." The labels Brian used (other than "dumb") could surely have been applied to himself as well. As Dr. Jordan (1992) has confirmed, "A child who has ADHD can be delightful . . . in a one-to-one situation, when he or she must enter a group and interact . . . a critical breakdown occurs. Inattention makes it impossible for these individuals . . . to put self aside in the interests of others" (p. 38).

Children with ADHD seem not to care about the effect they're having on others. We often carefully explained to Brian why certain actions would cause his classmates to shun him. Even after being disciplined, he didn't seem to understand what he'd done to annoy them. Brian usually cast the blame onto them. I'm not sure if he believed that or if it was a coverup for his own feelings of inadequacy.

Teaching social skills to a youngster with attention deficits can be very much like training a typical 2-year-old. I personally had a hard time living with the *same* "2-year-old" for several years in a row. It was frustrating and exhausting for Mark and me. By the time

Brian was finally growing out of this stage, our next son, Craig, was entering the "terrible twos."

It saddened Mark and me, and especially my mother, that Brad and Brian could not spend time together amiably. Brian had no other friends; the few neighbor children were not his age, and he had not made friends in school.

His sole playmate was his older brother, Brad. (Craig was still too young.) Brian's lack of other friends put pressure on Brad to always be available when Brian wanted him, though Brian did not usually reciprocate. It also meant Brian needed much more attention from Mark and me than the average child would.

Whenever we had to discipline the boys for their actions, Brian would cry out, "He started it!" or "Why didn't you tell me that would happen?" when he fully knew the consequences. Avoiding punishment and displacing blame are typical childish reactions, but Brian almost always responded that way.

Once Brian started school, it did not take long before most children simply left him alone. My heart ached in knowing that Brian was wandering the playground alone. Yet when he did have chances to join in the play, he usually did not respond. That baffled me. Perhaps he didn't have confidence in himself or had learned to avoid groups because he'd not had a record of being successful.

One night we all attended a school dinner. Brian was irritable. Mark and I were tense, trying to maintain control and avoid confrontation. We made it through the serving line by keeping the boys separated. I kept Brian close to me, which was our usual arrangement. I often initiate conversation with his classmates in hopes Brian will join in; that night I knew better than to try. He made rude and negative comments about nearly everyone and everything there. We warned him that those remarks would have to stop. They did—for a full 5 minutes.

When he started up again, I told him to leave the lunchroom and go to the car. Mark and I felt angry, since our attendance at the meal was intended mostly for Brian's benefit. We were surprised that Brian did not resist at all. He seemed not to care if his peers saw him being reprimanded. When we rejoined him at the car, he wasn't disturbed. Being alone in the car was more comfortable for him than being in the crowded lunchroom.

That same evening, I crawled in bed with him for awhile. He was still irritable, and I wanted to settle him down. As soon as we were alone, one-on-one, Brian cuddled up as sweetly as can be. We had a very nice, close conversation about God and the planets; Brian hugged me tightly. How could such a dear child be such a demon at times?

In first grade Brian liked to help classmates who were of a minority group; some did not yet speak English well. He spoke with them on the playground but rarely joined in their games. I was pleased that he showed kindness toward them and told him so. I think that Brian felt confident in approaching them because they, too, were at a disadvantage in the classroom.

Birthdays found me planning parties at Brian's request and scrambling to find enough people to invite. Brad and Craig made two; Grandma was three, and Mark and I brought it to five. The neighbor girls were always invited, though they were 4 and 6 years younger than Brian. At my encouragement, he would name a class-mate that I could invite.

I took a picture each time Brian had a friend over, special occasion or not. His playing with someone his age was a rare event, maybe once per school year. As each new school year approaches, the child with ADHD faces new challenges; finding and keeping friends are important ones.

In second grade Brian had a friend his age, at last. Brian's speech therapist at school notified me of his help-fulness toward another boy who attended speech therapy with Brian. Jeff had special needs, too, and was extremely shy. The speech therapist tried to draw them together at school; I talked about Jeff at home and encouraged Brian to spend time with Jeff. I was elated at the prospect of a friend for Brian.

Brian told Mark one day, "Dad, I think Jeff is good for me. When I am with him, I don't get into as much trouble." His was an innocent but astute observation. Brian was actually doing something structured with another child, instead of wandering around and getting into the middle of conflicts or being the target of others' antics. On several days when Brian complained about trouble on the playground, we found out that Jeff had been absent from school. There seemed to be a direct correlation.

Jeff had developed a friendship with another boy. Brian took no interest in becoming a threesome, even at the expense of possibly losing Jeff's friendship. I invited the two boys to our house one afternoon. Brian played well for 15 minutes or so and then simply left the two in the yard together and went into the house and ignored them. They were confused. He would not go back outside, even when I insisted. I explained that they were his guests, and they might not want to come back if he did not treat them well. Brian shrugged and said, "I don't care." I knew he did, but why couldn't he act accordingly? How exasperating!

Brian and Jeff continued to play together throughout second grade, though nearly all their meetings were arranged by me or Jeff's mother. Neither of the boys would initiate getting together.

For a few weeks early that spring, Brian talked about games that he and Jeff had been playing: running races and tossing wood chips at a target. This was the first time we had heard of Brian's involving himself in creative and cooperative activities. Brian sounded lighthearted when he talked. That was music to my ears and relief to my worried heart.

Jeff joined us to celebrate Brian's 8th birthday. When the boys parted that day, Brian told Jeff to call him soon. A week passed with no call. We called Jeff but got no answer, so we taped a note to the door of his house. Another week passed, and it was still there.

Brian approached me about seeing Jeff. I was busy, so suggested he walk to another boy's house to see if he had heard from Jeff. Brian surprised me by his willingness to go there; he usually needed to be prodded into such an assertive move. I knew he was truly concerned that Jeff had not contacted him. Minutes later, Brian returned with a long face. "Jeff is moving," he informed me. "They are leaving today. He didn't even tell me so we could do something special together first." Brian felt deserted. I comforted him then; I cried later. Brian had lost his first and only true friend.

I suggested that he call another classmate or the boys his age now living across the street, but Brian repeatedly declined. He no longer had excuses of their rudeness or "dumbness" but simply was more comfortable alone. A child with ADHD who has a poor track record of socializing often chooses to play alone rather than risk the effort of getting along with others. Probably his closest buddy was the neighbor's dog. Brian spent a lot of time playing and talking with Mollie, whose unconditional "love" was just what Brian needed.

Brad and Brian were now getting along much better than before when they were younger. They were friends and playmates rather than just battling brothers. Brian was at times patient with Craig, now 3, and loved to teach him new things. Craig was not always patient with Brian, though! We now had more conflicts between Brian and Craig than between Brian and Brad. But overall, family life was bearable and often even pleasant. When the boys played and truly enjoyed one another, Mark and I made sure to praise them; our hearts glowed. A few times I cut out some paper award "ribbons," and pinned them to the boys' shirts (see Figure 11.1).

At the start of third grade, Brian still had no one else he could call a friend. But he began to join in group activities on the playground and to interact in the classroom. Brian became friends with two other boys. Their friendship did not last long, but we were encouraged by his willingness to reach out to a different classmate for companionship. This sign was small but significant; his self-esteem was now high enough to withstand and rebound after rejection.

What person without a friend can maintain a high regard of himself? What child without a playmate feels loved and wanted? What parent would not cry, at least inside, when his child repeatedly and justifiably says, "Nobody will play with me"?

Just as it is not easy to live with a child with ADHD, it cannot be easy to be that child's playmate. "The ADHD child puts a great deal of pressure upon those who must share his or her space," stated Dr. Jordan (1992, p. 10).

Figure 11.1. Example of "Good Brother" award.

At the same time, the child feels pressured by others invading (as he sees it) *his* space. It can be a catch-22, an endless cycle of futility and loneliness.

Brian told us one day of others teasing him at school about falling and flinging himself around (which he did often at home). Then he added, "But that was the old me. I don't do that anymore." He was at least becoming aware of his effect on others and proud of his social advances.

Mark, Brian, and I enrolled in a social skills group for children with ADHD at the clinic. The effectiveness of that type of therapy has been questioned, but it helped Brian to know he is not the only one with his difficulties. Dr. O— worked with the children on specific skills for difficult situations, such as what to do when someone teases them. All skills were based on the following general plan:

1. Stop! What is the problem?
2. What are some plans?
3. What is the best plan?
4. Do the plan.
5. Did the plan work?

The whole idea was to get the child into the habit of stopping to think before acting—to curb his impulsivity in favor of a controlled response. This plan gives him those important extra seconds to consider alternatives and respond in a more socially acceptable way than if he had acted on first impulse. The same steps can be used for such situations as responding to teasing, not interrupting, or managing anger.

Again, it was up to us parents to practice the plan daily. Only in this way could the skills become a habit. At first Brian resisted what he called "the stupid baby plan." But we persisted, and he was soon caught up in it.

He even taught it to his little brother, Craig. The plan is a good tool for teaching the boys to think ahead and to take responsibility for their actions.

As the months and years progressed, we would find ourselves needing to adapt this plan, add others, and always be prepared to work on whatever was going awry at the time.

By his late elementary and early middle school years, Brian was rarely disruptive in the classroom or on the playground. He now carried his struggles inside himself and became somewhat withdrawn (though he "let it all out" when he got home!). He was pleasant enough to his classmates but would neither initiate nor reciprocate social contact.

A classmate made several telephone calls and visits to our home. I was thrilled and thought Brian would be, too. But Brian disturbed and angered me by his lack of willingness (or was it lack of ability?) to greet this boy or spend more than a few minutes talking before he made up an excuse to retreat. A year later another boy whom Brian had met in band showed interest in being Brian's friend. This time Brian did show a desire and even attempted to call him once but did not reach him, and the boy eventually turned to others for friendship. During this time Brian showed new anxiety about school, his health, and even a new fear of the dark. He was almost phobic of personal interaction with peers—he would literally turn pale at the thought. A few visits with Dr. O—, much encouragement from Mark and me, and our request for extra guidance from the school staff helped him through that period.

Though Brian still prefers to spend time alone or with our family, he is less uncomfortable than before about being out in the world. He will occasionally come home from school and say, "I met someone who might be my friend" or "A kid who used to be my enemy was nice to me today." So he is exploring the idea of friendship and is slowly making progress in the social arena.

Parents, teachers, and anyone in regular contact with the child with ADHD can help him develop social awareness. The child is struggling with so many results of his disorder that he cannot break the circle of solitude he finds has enveloped him. They can help him reach out to others and teach him practical skills in making friends and in *being* a friend. Once he gains confidence and a sense of worth, the child can escape that circle of despair and reach out beyond himself. Only then will he know the joy and satisfaction of sharing himself with another human being.

Public Reactions 12.

Regulated, structured environments such as stores, restaurants, and churches will restrict any child. They demand attentiveness that exceeds the limits of even an older child with ADHD. As the environment gets tedious or boring for these children, they create their own stimulation, thus becoming distracting and annoying to others.

"Taking a hyperactive child out in public can be exhausting and embarrassing. Even older hyperactive children often seem compelled to touch and handle everything they see," stated Barbara Ingersoll, author of *Your Hyperactive Child* (1988, p. 8).

Mark and I often disagree on how much to expect of Brian's behavior in public places. Dr. Ingersoll suggested: "Make your expectations fit the child, not the other way around" (p. 11). Parents should keep in mind not what he *should* be able to do but what he *can* do. My interpretation of this seems too lenient for Mark; I usually think he is expecting too much. This problem is not a major conflict but does create some tension and argument between us.

Any structured social situation almost guarantees conflict between a child with ADHD and others. Though structure is the cornerstone in behavioral treatment, it is structure specifically geared toward the child's needs. The child who is put into a social situation that is regulated in a general way feels confined and often reacts in a socially improper way. Brian usually becomes loud and rude and flings himself about. He seems unaware of others' reactions to his peculiar behaviors.

I have refused to be embarrassed by anything Brian has done in public—embarrassed for him perhaps, but not for me, which does not mean I am never disappointed in his behavior or even angered by it. I've found that if I don't make an issue of minor incidents, they will usually pass without conflict. But if I chastise Brian, he will become loud and resistant, which is more disruptive to people around us than the original misbehavior was. I don't believe in letting my children get away with things, but sometimes it is so hard to tell whether Brian really can control a certain behavior. So, to punish or not? Mark and I constantly struggle with that.

Eating out, attending ball games, going to church or the park—all can be potential catastrophes. The child with ADHD can turn the most commonplace activity into a major event.

Going to church was hell, if I may say so! Mark would hold Craig (then a baby) while I kept Brad and Brian on opposite ends of the pew. Brian would wiggle and jiggle, be up and down, and pull at my sleeve or bump me endlessly. The only way to gain anything from the service was to steel myself and ignore him. Maybe I should have insisted on his sitting still, but whenever I tried he protested loudly. I felt he would be less disturbing to others if he was quiet. No matter how often or how I tried to still him, it never seemed to work for more than 3 minutes at a time.

There were smiles and comments: "You've got your hands full" and "They're all boy, aren't they?" I'd smile back and say, "They sure are." I got into the habit of calling them "the troops" or shrugging and saying "three boys" in mock exasperation. I saw knowing looks behind the smiles, thinking, "He sure is a busy one" or "Wonder what his problem is?" Sometimes I longed to announce to all what we were dealing with. I wanted the whole world to know why Brian had difficulties and to recognize and understand other children with similar problems.

One day I was to read Scriptures in church. Brian and Brad were along, not Mark. They were getting along well and sitting quite still, so I got up in front at the proper time. As soon as my reading started, out of the corner of my eye I saw them tussling. I was helpless; I could not leave until I was done, but I didn't want them to disrupt others and become noisy. Brian's Sunday school teacher was sitting near them; she did the perfect thing—put Brian on her lap, locked her arms around him, and held on tight. He struggled, but she did not let go, and I was free to concentrate on my task. I was so grateful to her for making that decision and knowing firmness was called for.

Most people are sensitive and caring when I explain our situation (though I suppose I tend to share it most readily with those from whom I anticipate a warm response). I do not ask for sympathy, just empathy and understanding.

Everyone can relate to the screaming child in the grocery cart. All eyes are on Mom. They're thinking, "Why doesn't she do something?" Some would want him spanked; others would view that as abuse. Some would want him removed, some scolded, still others ignored. Part of parenting is deciding the best method of treating a difficult situation. Parents of children with ADHD are faced with more difficult decisions than most parents.

I remember Brian lying on the floor in the aisle of a department store—just lying there scowling at the ceiling for no apparent reason. His big brother was embarrassed. Do I ignore Brian or demand that he get up when I know my insistence will cause him to make a scene? I chose to stand and wait him out. Many people walked by with wondering looks. I maintained a firm, controlled stance, not entering into oral combat with my son. He eventually got up and proceeded as normal.

It is important and extremely helpful for parents of a child with ADHD to receive support from others around them. Little things mean a lot: an offer to baby-sit for an hour, a smile in the midst of a crisis, even just being nonjudgmental can in itself be a positive stroke.

Another situation that caused tension for Mark and me was taking the boys to Mark's evening softball games. I would spend most of my time watching to be sure they were safe, as well as not hurting or annoying anyone else. Between that and conversing with friends, I was lucky to catch a few plays of the game! The hassle of getting the boys ready (usually without cooperation) and dealing with them throughout the hour made it hardly worth going. Yet at least I did get out, and Mark appreciated our being there.

When Craig was a toddler, I used an expandable strap connecting his wrist to mine so that he could not go far. He was free to play and move around without my worrying about him getting onto the field or into the street. I wish I would have done the same for the other boys, especially Brian. I did get a few looks as if I was walking my dog, but most mothers commented that it was a good idea. It added to my peace of mind and did not hinder Craig's ability to play.

After the ball games, when the players and families would gather, most of Mark's teammates would greet the boys with boisterous hellos. They would toss them into the air or engage in mock boxing. Their intentions were fine, but this type of action would just fuel Brian for aggressive, hyperactive behaviors of his own. Once started, he was not able to slow down. Often he would get carried away and become a real nuisance until I had to take him home.

Our society accepts, and even expects, boisterous play from boys; Mark and I, even before Brian's troubles, have preferred to nurture rather than overstimulate our children. For Brian, these aggressive approaches from others was fuel for his fire. Mark and I tried to explain our concerns to our closest friends, but we were not comfortable in asking everyone else to stop the "man-to-man" approach. It always fostered aggressiveness in Brian. He would inevitably end up in trouble, though he hadn't started it. Yet those who had started it had done so unaware of the consequences.

The individual with ADHD does not choose these particular problems any more than someone chooses deafness or diabetes or his eye color. Brian is learning to understand the disorder and deal with its effects on his life.

One thing I never let myself worry about is if others wonder why I can't control Brian's behavior. Knowing I am doing the best I can, I put on blinders and desensitize myself. The best I can show others is that I accept and love him as he is.

A Father's View 13.

Mark Neuville

When I read excerpts from Maureen's book, I flash back to some of the horrors of the past. I remember our telephone ringing, and the results were the same as the opening bell of a boxing match. *Mom's on the phone, she's busy, I can get away with belting my brother.* I remember the times of trying to get out of the house and to work on time and still have my sanity, and ending up at work with neither!

It was apparent from an early age that Brian was quite different from our first child and that our techniques for discipline definitely had to change. Brian would wake up with his "motor running" in high gear, and it would almost be impossible to slow him down. How I wish we could have hidden a video camera and filmed Brian in action to show people what it was like around our house!

How thankful we are to have more control and a better grasp of how to live peacefully with a child with ADHD.

I must thank Maureen for helping us get as far as we are. She took it on herself to dig deep into Brian's troubles until we found a direction to head. I'm the type to tough it out, wait it out, try to tackle the problem by myself. But we couldn't handle it. Since counseling, we can—most of the time. There is also a social stigma about having to see a psychiatrist or psychologist. But after living like we did for those 3 years, I knew we couldn't change things on our own.

It was a blessing to have Brian diagnosed as having ADHD and start on a program to learn how to live in peace and harmony. The time we've spent with Brian's psychologist has been quite helpful. She makes us realize what we are dealing with and how to plan a course of action. We learned (and are still learning) what Brian is dealing with.

I was not in favor of Brian's taking medication at first. I do not believe in taking medicines unless absolutely necessary. This *is* a case of it being absolutely necessary. The benefits definitely outweigh the potential side effects. Brian still has a favorable response to his medication. Some days I can see a dramatic change in behavior when the medicine "kicks in." But medicine alone cannot cure all society's ills.

There was a 3-month period between first and second grade when we took Brian off the medication. He seemed to function OK, though he was not quite as manageable. After a month of school, concerns about Brian's behavior and schoolwork started, so we went back to the medication. It had positive results.

Why did that 3-month period go smoothly, and why can't it be that way all the time? Maybe because summertime is a time when there is less structure than during school. There are less demands on his time, more time to just wander and do as he pleases. In Brian's case a combination of medication and behavior management plans seems to be doing the trick.

I have mixed feelings on parents' support groups. If all we do is "cry in our beer" and complain about how rough things are, I don't want any part of it. We all have our horror stories, and I know we need to let our troubles come out in the open. But we need to do something about them. If we can share not only our struggles but also our techniques on how to handle these situations, I feel support groups can be of use to me. It's up to us parents to work with our children until these plans become a habit. It is work, but the rewards will be worth it.

We are involved in our local CH.A.D.D. chapter (CHildren and Adults with Attention Deficit Disorder), a national organization, which makes the general public aware of what ADHD is and provides support for parents and other people who come in contact with persons with ADHD. Our chapter has professionals give presentations on various aspects of ADHD: medical, home, and school issues.

Maureen and I have given presentations on the effects that ADHD has on a family's home life. Even though no two children with ADHD (or any children) are exactly alike, there are certain commonalities between most families' experiences with ADHD. We told our story, and people in the audience would cry, laugh, and nod their heads; we've all traveled much the same path. It's comforting to know we are not the only family to struggle with ADHD.

Maureen and I were involved in a group of parents with children from 8 to 10 years old. We met every 3 weeks, with the children meeting as often to learn about ADHD. We learned about the difficulties ADHD can present for children and behavioral management plans for when they have problems to solve. They were at the age to comprehend information about ADHD.

I can see how abuse can happen in a dysfunctional family living with a child with ADHD. The child who will not behave despite all warnings from the parent could easily become the scapegoat for other problems in the family. If the spousal relationship is not going well, living with a child with ADHD could be the "last straw" and cause one parent to walk out. Our relationship is not that way. Maureen and I have times when one of us is no longer under control. That person can then leave for a while, with the other one taking over in the meantime.

We each need to have our own way of coping and getting away from the hassles. I would work in the garden, shovel snow, or take a shower—anything so I wouldn't have to see or listen to Brian. When I get to that point, I just can't stand to listen to all the confusion in our house.

The school staff is aware of Brian's disorder, but he still has to follow the same rules as anyone else; that is as it should be. It is harder for him to comply, and he gets disciplined more often than most children. But we try not to foster a feeling of "I can get away with this because I have ADHD."

If someone in your school district suggests that a child of yours may have ADHD, please listen. However, teachers cannot diagnose the disorder. Let a trained professional and your conscience be the final judges. Make sure in your heart that you've exhausted the other possibilities and are not looking for an easy answer or a label for the problem.

Dealing with Brian's ADHD costs us a lot of time and money. Our insurance premiums are over $300 per month, and the insurance still covers less than half of Brian's medical expenses. But juvenile delinquency and substance abuse problems would cost even more. Children with ADHD do have a greater likelihood of juvenile delinquency, substance abuse, and other undesirable consequences. It's like they say, "You can pay now, or you can pay later." I'd rather spend my time and money on preventing problems.

I've seen children who I'd bet my house on have ADHD but who are receiving no treatment. I feel sorry for them and their parents. The disorder doesn't go away in the majority of cases; sooner or later the disorder must be dealt with. It is unfair to the child and anyone around him to not do as much as can be done to help the child.

One of the toughest things about living with a child with ADHD is that his actions must almost always be monitored. Maureen and I cannot be together on the same level of the house with the kids on a different level. About 95% of the time, fights will occur within 30 seconds. Then one of us has to go and referee. This drives me nuts! Add that to the regular picking up after the kids, and I often felt like the person walking behind the parade horses with a scoop shovel—a thankless job!

It doesn't seem fair to have to constantly know what my children are doing, monitor their play and conversations, and intervene before warfare starts. I don't think it is fair, but it is necessary. We sometimes let them fight their own battles as long as it doesn't get out of hand. We try to help them settle their differences by talking instead of fighting. Sometimes this approach works. Sometimes it doesn't.

I finally got to the point where I can anticipate problems and stop them before they escalate. We have to constantly try to anticipate problems before they happen. Maureen reminds me of that often.

Now the kids can play for a long time without fighting. Thank God for those occasional breaks we receive. But the carefree times are much less often than for most families we are acquainted with. Parents with children with great physical and mental hardships very rarely receive breaks, and I feel for them. For them it is a constant problem. At least we get some breaks.

I am concerned about how Brian will be perceived by his peers in the coming years. I hope that he will succeed socially and not be shunned or end up an outcast. He recently said, "The kids make fun of me, but that was the old Brian they remember. I'm not like that anymore." He has made great strides socially. But it is hard for kids to change their opinions of another that they don't like. Kids give few second chances.

During third grade, kick ball was the main activity on the playground; that's usually the first thing I heard about when I saw him after school. Brian seemed to be accepted by the other children in those games. I believe it was a good activity for him. Kick ball was his big release of energy for the day. They played after lunch, after 3 to 4 hours of being bottled up in school, shortly after he took his second dose of medication, in the large, wide-open schoolyard, where he could get outside and just go!

He even talked about several friends he made playing kick ball. Brian had one over to our house, and it went great. They did things that are common for most children his age but are much more difficult for children with ADHD. We didn't have to constantly monitor them, as we normally would have. The two boys even sat up on top of the swing set for 15 minutes looking at spiderwebs and talking about creepy, crawly things! This was a wonderful experience for all of us.

My main concerns now are about the future. Brian is a bright and charming kid. If he channels his energies in a positive direction, he will do fine. He has a disorder that he didn't ask for and that is hard for him to cope with at times.

What happens if the medication is no longer effective? I hope that Brian will have developed enough self-control, common sense, and discipline to thrive in the real world and that the behavioral management skills we work on will be ingrained enough in his mind to help him through. In the sanctuary of our home we can guide him along. When he is on his own we won't be able to.

If he is having an argument with someone on a stairway, will Brian be able to stop himself before he shoves him down the stairs? These kids are very impulsive. They act before they think. When Brian gets in trouble, usually he can see how his actions got him into trouble after we explain it to him. But he doesn't retain what we tell him as often as the average child. Minutes later he will do the same thing, get in the same trouble, and wonder why. If he is having a disagreement with a teacher or an employer, will he have the discipline not to tell him off and get into deeper trouble but be able to diplomatically resolve their dispute?

It will be more difficult than for most children for Brian to succeed. Thankfully Brian was diagnosed at a relatively young age, and he is receptive to the behavior management skills we try to teach him. But it will be a constant struggle for him, and we will help him all that we can. ADHD is a disorder that does not go away but must be dealt with one instance and one day at a time. If we keep working with Brian like we have and Brian keeps working with us, we hope he will do just fine.

Other Family Problems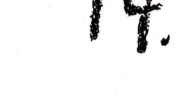

For the family, attention deficits and hyperactivity can have far-reaching repercussions. As Barbara Ingersoll (1988) has described it, "Like a pebble tossed into a pond, the hyperactive child's problems cause ripples that extend far beyond the child himself" (p. 117).

Sibling Conflict

Conflicts are a normal part of life, but the strain of Brian's special needs creates additional stress and conflict for us. When Brian was younger, there were weeks when Mark and I felt all we did was struggle with discipline and settle conflicts. Most were between the boys, either Brian and Brad or Brian and Craig. Mark and I had our share, too, usually over discipline and our expectations of Brian. We had all become argumentative.

I have always stressed talking about and working out problems. Physical conflict, rather than verbal, bothers me most. Sometimes it was impossible to separate which struggles were due to Brian's disorder and which to the fact that they were three young, active, and very determined boys.

In those "awful years," the boys would trip and poke and hit and wrestle with each other. Some days we seemed to be constantly pulling them apart. No sort of discipline (time-outs, explanations, threats, or spankings) would curb their behavior for more than a few minutes. They seemed determined to go right back to it.

Noncompliance itself can be aggravating to any parent. Add the child's refusal to stop the actions and a lack of remorse, and it leaves a parent very frustrated and angry. These are the times when Mark and I feel helpless and ineffective as parents.

Brian's noncompliance was one of the most difficult things for Mark and me to accept. Our requests were constantly defied or ignored; we felt frustrated and not in control of our own household. "Noncompliance has . . . serious ramifications for later behavior and parent-child relationships," wrote Marilyn T. Erickson in *Behavior Disorders of Children and Adolescents* (1983).

Some mornings I tried to keep track of how many outbursts or conflicts required my intervention. I once wrote it down so I know it was, at times, every 5 minutes. That pace would slacken; the first hour or two upon arising were the hardest. Brian seems to need time to adjust to any new situation; each new morning can be disturbing for him.

While Brian's behaviors precipitated most of the boys' confrontations, we tried to not always put the primary blame on Brian. Yet it was very hard not to blame him when he was continually doing things that were annoying and improper.

Mark and I hated to always be reprimanding the boys, yet we could not allow them to continue misbehaving. If we had remained consistent and brought each impropriety to their attention, they would have been under constant discipline. But to break the cycle of negativism, we sometimes chose to let incidents go without comment. Deciding which behaviors to penalize and which to let go presented a fine line to balance. Mark developed a good rule that anything concerning health or safety must be taken care of. Beyond that, it was a matter of parental choice. The biggest problem then was that the parents (Mark and I) often did not agree!

We tried to tell Brad not to cry or strike back at Brian's attacks but to ignore him and walk away. In theory this would have given Brian no reinforcement or no pleasure from his actions and eventually curb his aggressive behavior. In practice it was impossible and probably unfair to expect of 8-year-old Brad.

Brad has experienced anger and frustration from putting up with his brother. We have occasionally taken Brad to Brian's psychologist so Brad could express his own concerns. It helped Brad to be told that it was normal for him to have trouble coping. He was also more tolerant knowing that Brian did not always act as he did on purpose. Like most big brothers, Brad can also be very protective of and helpful toward Brian.

When Craig was a baby and in his infant seat, if I would leave the house long enough to get him strapped in the car, the other two would be rolling on the floor and fighting by the time I came back to the house. If I would take the two youngest to the car first, Brian would be torturing Craig by the time I made another trip back to the house. The only effective way to work it out was to keep Brian with me at all times, which sometimes meant he would have to make several trips to and from the car with me. But at least I would be able to maintain control over the situation.

Some days I would have to exercise this system several times a day—each time I left the house or picked them up at school or day care or went to do errands. It got old in a hurry. It also slowed me down, which I could not afford to do some mornings. When I would try to get by again without the structured plan, they would invariably end up fighting.

Once, after a confrontation with his brother, Brian came running to me wildly and cried, "Mom, the trouble with mornings is that you have to protect me." He, like most children with ADHD, sees everyone else as attacking him and invading his space rather than the other way around.

Just remembering all those struggles makes me feel tense. All that consistency, structure, and patience can be such a chore. Mark is naturally consistent and tried to maintain structure, but his usual patience was worn thin. I am an organized person but inconsistent. I'm usually quite tolerant of the boys' actions and can cope for some time, then fall apart all at once.

Mark and I, in our tiredness, did tend to curtail even some normal childlike activities. We were so sick of noise and confusion that we stifled any attempts at boisterous play. We rarely let them wrestle or bicker even if it seemed harmless. Though we tired of intervening, we continued to do it. Experience showed us that nonintervention resulted in chaos. We hope they will still learn to settle their differences.

One time I decided Brad and Brian ought to settle their own conflict. I calmly picked them up between "tackles" and put them in their bedroom. They were to calm down before they came back downstairs. The battle was resumed as soon as I left. Within 3 minutes I was on my way to the emergency room; Brian needed four stitches. So much for settling their own battles!

I have complained that our first two sons, Brian in particular, rarely engaged in creative play. They didn't enjoy Legos or other building toys. Since Brian disliked coloring, he was not artistically creative. I would try to initiate interest in acting, making up stories, or building a tent. If they would respond at all, the interest was short-lived. Since we could rarely leave them together for fear of confrontation, their lack of relaxed time together probably curbed any creative inclinations.

As Brad entered middle and high school, he was often gone from home for after-school activities. Brian and

Craig now spent time together, often having fun. But most of their interactions would still end in rolling on top of and hitting each other. Mark and I needed to intervene as much as we had earlier with Brian and Brad.

The results of our discipline were in some ways unfair. Sometimes I wish we could have just let them be kids and not have to constantly monitor and manipulate them. Looking back, though, we couldn't have done things much differently. Constant structure is what the child with ADHD will resist but needs the most.

Marital Stress

Brian was 4 when his hyperactivity and attentional problems became serious. That same fall Craig was born.

Our first two children had never slept all night until they were at least 6 months old; Craig followed suit. I have always needed a lot of sleep. After getting up in the night at least once with Craig, and Brian bounding in anywhere from 5:30 a.m. on, I never felt rested.

During the next 2 years, Mark and I were so tired we could hardly function some days. We were both exhausted from the strain of trying to manage Brian's behavior, as well as the worry over what, if anything, was really wrong. Mark and I shared the burden of getting up early and spent most weekends catching up on sleep. We would literally take turns napping. Most days I would be so drained (physically and emotionally) that by the time the last of the boys was in bed, I would drop. It was not uncommon for me to be asleep by 8:30 p.m. I know now that part of the constant tiredness was due to stress and depression.

Because we were both suffering from stress and exhaustion, we could each understand how the other felt. Though we had few reserves to draw from, we did try to cater to the other when we felt a need to sleep or just get away for a while. It often came down to who was "merely" tired and who was truly exhausted!

I knew that Mark was under as much duress as I; he knew the same about me. Yet we often vented our frustrations on each other. Unfair as it was, we needed to release them somehow, and I think that we knew our harsh words were largely a cover-up for the fears we harbored in our hearts. Our tolerance was low and tempers were short, but we usually got over our hurts quickly. We could at least understand where the other was coming from, and we tried to talk over our differences and work them out.

Strained as we were, it was difficult for Mark and me to be pleasant with one another. We often felt tired and harassed and wanted nothing more than to be left alone, which was not conducive to marital closeness or intimacy. We had times of great resentment and anger at having to live through this. Often we took these problems out on the children and on each other by being just plain grumpy.

At first we frequently disagreed over how to discipline the children. Our values are basically the same, but we go about achieving them in different ways. We did for a time disagree in front of the children but soon realized we needed to back up each other's decisions even when we weren't in full agreement. Once we got into counseling and using our behavior modification techniques, we complemented each other pretty well.

Children with ADHD almost always generate stress, anger, and frustration within a family. Therapy helped us reduce some of this wear and tear. Parents of children with ADHD, and mothers in particular, often have feelings of guilt, depression, and loneliness.

All in all, our family has done pretty well, I think. Even when troubled, Brian feels secure in coming back to one of us for reassurance. His early school drawings reflected this strong sense of family identity. Nearly all of

Brian's drawings were of us, his family, or our house. One of his early teachers noticed this and commented on it; she suggested it was because he felt secure with us.

Within the family, and especially on a one-to-one basis, Brian can be sweet and sincere. He is affectionate and open about expressing his thoughts and feelings. Even when he is hurt or angry he can express them in a uniquely poignant way. I had once sent him to his room for misbehavior and remember that he was unusually apologetic. A letter he wrote to me conveys his sense of feeling his actions were out of his control (see Figure 14.1).

Special Events

A child with ADHD can turn almost any everyday event into a chaotic situation. Mealtime with a hyperactive child is anything but peaceful. Because of Brian's sensitivity, he would often get upset about noises or motions one of us was making. That would put us all on edge. He usually sat on the edge of his chair with both feet swinging; he would thwart his own attempts at eat-

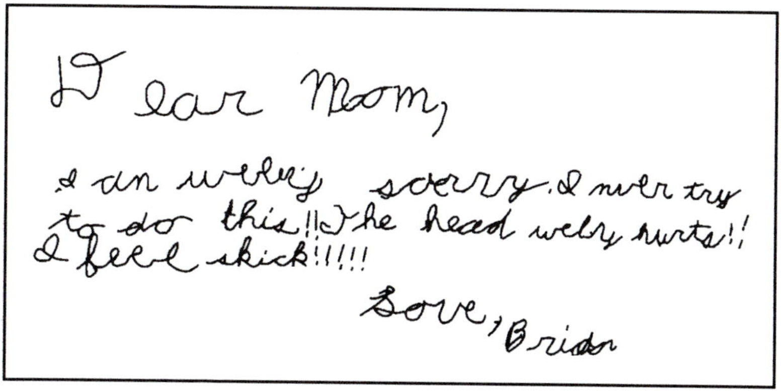
Dear Mom,

I an velry sorry. I nver try to do this!! The head velry hurts!! I feel skick!!!!!

Love, Brian

Figure 14.1. Brian's apology.

ing by fumbling the fork. After retrieving it, he'd start the process once more, usually needing to leave his chair several times to pick up something he had dropped. Up, down, up, down.

Trying to get a shoe on Brian or his arm in the shirtsleeve was like hitting a moving target. He never stood still; he resisted or ran away nearly every time; he would wiggle and fling himself around. He frequently banged his head into mine or flung his hand into my face. Both actions annoyed and angered me. I finally thought of standing him on a stool in the middle of the room. I would stand at arm's length (mine, not his) and pick up one foot to place it in his pants or shoe. He had no choice but to stand still or he would fall. After all that, it would be hard to be in the proper mood to take him and the other boys out. Our processions to and from the car to get them all settled took more time and effort; then I still had to keep them under control in the car, not to mention what I might face when I'd arrive at our destination!

Almost any outing with a child with special needs takes extra planning and effort and still has a good chance of going awry. Picnics, dining out, concerts, school functions, ball games, church, or any restrictive situation requires parents to be keenly aware of the child and how he is reacting to his surroundings.

We also needed to keep Brian's medication in mind, timing some activities around his peak hours of compliance and attentiveness.

We have found that we need to keep holidays and other special events simple and low-key. Talking for weeks ahead and getting the boys excited about Christmas, for example, just makes them highly impatient and excitable. Brian especially does not handle this excitement well, which is not uncommon for children with ADHD.

On a family birthday, I asked Brian to decorate the cake. Grandma helped. Brian put the candles on, but

Grandma straightened them. Brian went wild, "You messed it up!" We calmed him down. I instinctively knew Brian would want to carry the cake to the table, but Mark had already done it. Brian stamped upstairs, screaming, out of control. I went up and held Brian to calm him down; he stopped his tirade and rejoined us. The first word anyone uttered he stamped off crying, "Now you've seen the cake and ruined the surprise." By now everyone was tense and obviously not celebrating anymore. We proceeded carefully, some of us holding back tears, trying just to get through the "Happy Birthday" song with no more scenes. I can't imagine what was going on in Brian's mind throughout this time, not to mention the flow of others' emotions caused by such an outbreak.

At times like this I wish I could lash out, but that would only make things worse. A parent of a child with ADHD must constantly guide and mediate, which is stressful and exhausting and creates inner resentment.

Halloween is no "hallowed evening" at our house! Even in elementary school, Brian balked at preparing a costume and said that he didn't want to "be" anything. I had to gently prod him into agreeing on something (sometimes by threatening to make the decision myself).

The confusion and excitement of the evening proved too much for Brian. As we left the house, almost anyone he saw or heard set him off. One year he lay on the sidewalk screaming, totally oblivious to what the other ghosts and goblins thought of him. Another year he ran to his room and refused to go trick-or-treating. His behavior, of course, angered his brothers, who cried or shouted at him. Mark got disgusted. I was angry, but I calmed Brian down enough to get him outside again. Once he began his trek and overcame the initial trauma, he proceeded and enjoyed himself.

Christmas and birthdays have often found Brian opening gifts with a frown or complaint. He has even angrily stated that a gift wasn't what he wanted, even if he had been waiting for it. He couldn't handle the excitement, and reacted adversely. We had to learn to accept that this is his way and wait him out quietly, and within a minute he was usually examining the gift with a smile on his face.

He received many gifts for his First Communion. Mark and I held our breaths at each opening for fear he would offend someone. God must have been truly with him that day, as he was as polite and appreciative as can be! We praised him for how well he handled it and how good he made the gift givers feel.

Before any special event, parents should consider attending the event at a time when the child's medication is at peak effectiveness. Parents should also anticipate problems, discuss them ahead of time with the child, and monitor the child throughout the event to see that he is handling the excitement appropriately. If there are situations that are difficult for a child to cope with and repeatedly cause problems, these events can be avoided entirely or the child may be left in a sitter's care. Everyone will be happier.

Baby-Sitters

One of those not-so-obvious but fairly significant effects of ADHD on our lives has been the difficulty in getting and keeping baby-sitters. This is a common problem for parents of hyperactive children.

I have worked part time ever since our oldest son, Brad, was born. We changed daytime caregivers rather frequently; either we moved or I changed jobs or the sitters moved away. Brad did not seem to be affected much; he adapted quite easily.

I also had to change sitters frequently after Brian was born. Brian did not adjust to those changes as easily as

Brad had. By the time he was 2, I knew it would take a special person to care for him. Most sitters would agree to work with Brian, but some did not; others could not cope with him.

In one sitter's home, there was another boy about Brian's age who was very aggressive. I knew Brian felt threatened, and I did not like the way he was responding with aggression of his own. This situation did not precipitate Brian's misbehavior, but it did accentuate his problems.

On the other hand, I had a few wonderful caregivers. One sensed Brian's struggles on her first day with him. He was only a year old; I was hardly yet aware of his special needs. She was firm and consistent, yet caring and encouraging. I will always remember and appreciate her. Unfortunately, she moved out of town soon after we started with her.

We considered a day care center, but the cost was prohibitive and I did not always work a regular schedule. We also felt that Brian would be best nurtured in a home atmosphere with a single caregiver. Now that our third son is in a day care center, I think that Brian may have benefited from the structure of one, though he probably would have been unhappy having to interact in a group setting.

Evening baby-sitters have also been difficult to find and keep. We can not rely on girls in junior high or high school as most of our friends can. Most teenagers do not discipline children well; they are either uncomfortable doing it or they do not know how to discipline effectively. Our sitters learn about the disorder from us and how we expect them to deal with each misbehavior.

Our best source of evening sitters has been the nearby college, especially students in education or fields working with children with special needs. They have had some training or experience with difficult children and have the interest to work with them. However, they are busy with studies and regular jobs or go home for the summer and are often not available when we need them.

It would be difficult to find someone willing to handle three active boys anyway. Brian's ADHD made it harder, since all of them have heightened activity and aggression levels and low tolerance of one another. Some evenings they are a handful for Mark and me! There were times when we had to hire two sitters at once to keep things under control while we were gone.

The few times Mark and I get away gives us a break from our everyday hassles and a chance to renew our commitment to one another. Parents of children with ADHD need to get away on their own as much or more than any parents, and a single parent must find a babysitter to rely on so he or she can get away and have time alone or with other adults. Difficulty in getting adequate sitters compounds the problem.

Heartaches and Happiness

Every family has its ups and downs. A family dealing with ADHD probably has more than average, with the "ups" quite high and the "downs" very low. We deal with fear, guilt, panic, exhaustion, anger, resentment, and heartache regularly. We also are blessed with moments of joy, relief, hope, and pride.

I am ever thankful that Brian's disorder is not a physically threatening one and that we are working through it. We can always see children worse off. Mark and I try to keep this in mind, yet some days that thought doesn't lighten our load.

During the time Brian was 4 to 6 years old, he was an unhappy child. He said things like, "I'm not a part of this world, I'm just a machine," "I wish I had a different life," and "Nobody loves me, I'm no good." This kind of expression was no game of make believe; he was reaching out for help. I felt so sorry for this little boy who looked at the world so glumly.

My biggest heartaches come with seeing Brian's lack of friends and his lack of skills or even desire to make any. One vivid memory is from his early grade school years. I was near his school during the course of my workday and drove past the playground to see whether he was out. He was. I hoped to see him with other children—he was not. Brian was wandering around, sidestepping potential playmates, and looking forlorn. He stopped to sit at a picnic table, laid back on it, and studied the sky for a bit. Then he got up to wander again. He was not blissfully daydreaming. He was alone in a sea of children. I sat and cried, and my heart broke for him.

When given an opportunity to establish a friendship, Brian usually either ignores or is rude to the other child, which makes me angry, not so much at Brian, but at the disorder that makes socializing so difficult for him. Our efforts to encourage his social opportunities plus a social skills group at the clinic have helped Brian become more confident and receptive to others. He feels better about himself and enjoys life more, plus it takes a bit of the responsibility off Mark and me to be his sole providers of companionship.

It is still difficult dealing with Brian's impulsivity and distractibility. Mark and I find that we are even less tolerant now than before. We do not have to rigidly manage Brian's behavior anymore, so we find it annoying when we have to go back to those old tactics.

No family is without conflict or problems; I do not expect ours to be. We experience the same difficulties (sickness, job hassles, financial worries) as any family. But those kinds of things come and go. Our dealings with Brian's ADHD are continuous. When already stressed from these interactions, we find it harder to confront and deal with other problems.

For a couple of years Mark and I felt burdened by our worries over Brian's difficulties. We managed to get through some days simply because we had no choice but to keep going. Then Craig needed much of the same discipline as Brian did at that age. At times I felt genuine pain at having to relive those earlier days.

I often envied my friends whose children were, for the most part, compliant and manageable. I struggled to keep that envy from affecting my feelings about the friendship itself.

It all seemed so complex. I longed to live a simple, more hassle-free life. But Mark and I knew that our problems, unlike some, were not insurmountable.

As Brian grew and matured, he became more in control of himself, more aware of his difficulty with noises and lack of organization of his schoolwork. There were still times, however, when we're amazed at how he could still become forgetful, confused, and distraught over what seemed to us to be nothing at all.

But we could finally get through times without the conflicts and tensions that had haunted us for so long. They were once part of our everyday functioning; we finally broke the cycle. We've tackled ADHD head-on and discovered that with a multimodal treatment program (medical, behavioral, and educational interventions plus counseling), the disorder can be managed.

We truly appreciated and enjoyed the peace and harmony that many families take for granted. Having gone through hard times, we appreciated the good so much more.

Looking Ahead 15.

During the summer of Brian's 8th birthday, we finally had a sense of his growing up. Brian showed remarkable improvement in his social skills. His attitude in group situations was now participatory rather than aggressive. Others noticed and commented on his improvements.

While 4 and 5 years old, Brian had been physically aggressive toward others in his group (e.g., school and ball teams). At 6 and 7, Brian's aggressive behaviors were under control; he now stood back and observed rather than participated. By age 8, he participated, sometimes actively. He still chose not to reach out to others, but when they did to him, he would not shun them.

For the first time in three summers of playing on a ball team, Brian became attentive in the field and assertive at getting the ball. He did not complain about his teammates bothering him. His aggressions were replaced by cooperation.

At a city festival that summer, Brian and Craig were waiting in line for a ride. Mark and I observed Brian speaking to the child in front of him. We looked at each other, our hearts glowing. It was rare that he'd engage in casual conversation with another child.

We saw many little signs of Brian's maturing. He often put aside anger for those first critical seconds and dealt with it in a less aggressive manner than before. He seemed to care more for others; up until now he had been oblivious to anyone else's feelings.

I could actually leave Brad and Brian together in a room for some time, and they would play amicably. It was wonderful to see the brothers enjoying one another instead of battling.

We now laughed out loud at Brian's antics and joked around with him without crushing his self-image. When Brian wasn't "hyper" and into trouble, we did not have to make as many requests for him to comply. With fewer requests, there were fewer chances for him to resist and therefore fewer conflicts. As the tension subsided, Mark and I became more calm, which helped keep Brian and his brothers on the right track.

Our reprieve was short-lived. Just when Brian became "under control," Craig began to act out. Craig seemed to be imitating his older brother. Well, we were used to behavior charts, so we just kept right on doing them with Craig.

Brian's third-grade report card reflected his progress. His academic skills earned him A's and B's with only one C. More important to Mark and me, his effort and attitude grades were now satisfactory to excellent. (In past years these had been satisfactory or needed improvement.) He was beginning to open up and contribute ideas in class. As we sat in conference with Brian's teacher, Mark and I glowed with pleasure. She suggested a few areas in which Brian could exert more effort, but for that night we simply wanted to rest on his laurels and feel proud of him.

Brian would now finally hop on his bike and explore the neighborhood or go to the nearby park on his own and find new activities. He still played alone and preferred it that way, but he began to act more like an average boy his age. In school he wasn't often picked on or shunned like before, but he remained somewhat of a loner. I still worried about Brian but tried to focus on his progress and praise him for it.

Meanwhile, Craig became more and more annoying. He even acted out in some of the ways that Brian had at the same age (3 to 4 years). That was scary, since Brian had ceased some of those actions before Craig was even born. I had the thought that Craig might have ADHD as well, but he was so much unlike Brian. Craig was creative and industrious and not forgetful as Brian could be. So Mark and I kept on plugging with Craig—we were used to busy boys!

For the next few years Brian did fairly well in school. Much of his success could be attributed to our continued work at home, frequent communications with his teachers, and the teachers' willingness to support us and guide Brian. He was no longer disruptive in school but was viewed as a quiet child. (At home, however, he was still Brian!) His social development remained "on hold"; he made few, if any, attempts to establish even casual friendships.

Brian's fifth-grade teacher both challenged and encouraged Brian; our son blossomed under his direction. The best thing that came of that experience is that Brian gained a sense of competence and confidence in himself.

Meanwhile, Craig busied himself at home, cutting paper and taping the pieces together, tying strings and making inventions, cooking and creating endlessly. Craig, like his brothers, loved playing cards and doing anything with numbers. He was bright beyond his years and intuitive as well. I recognized early on that Craig needed to be challenged and kept busy to be happy.

Craig wore me out physically and emotionally in trying to keep up with him. He was insistent and persistent; he was insatiable. Craig never gave up on anything— and he asked for a lot! (He had earned the nickname "Craiger Beggar.") He also talked incessantly. He was even more intense than Brian had been and more constantly active. Craig could be such a sweetheart—usually delightful—but he would show his dark side suddenly and severely.

Despite our efforts to modify his behavior, Craig became less and less compliant; unlike Brian, he actually refused our requests. We again had a hard time getting sitters to come back and care for the boys. Mark and I once again became frustrated and resentful. Our upward cycle was beginning to slip back downward again.

Mark and I worried and wondered if this son, too, had ADHD, but again we thought it might be a stage. We were adamant about making sure that Craig was not automatically pegged with the same label as Brain had been. We talked with Dr. O—, who encouraged us to keep up our methods and to let her know if Craig's behavior became too disruptive. Deep in my heart I knew what was wrong but could not bring myself to admit it. This time we *were* in denial.

Then, when Craig was barely 5 years old, we were asked to remove him from his daytime care center because of his unruly and aggressive behavior. This was the final blow. I called Dr. O— and asked her what we already knew: What were the chances of having a second child with ADHD? She said there is a strong possibility, and she recommended we bring Craig in for evaluation. We did, and his assessment strongly showed that he "had it."

We were devastated. I think we went through the motions of behavior modification plans and the like, but my heart was not in his treatment for some months. I was usually one to call friends and family, talk things over, cry, and get on with life, but I did not share this news as readily. I was grieving.

Even after knowing how helpful medication had been for Brian, Mark and I decided to wait to medicate Craig. Again, we wanted to be sure it was necessary and that we were not taking the easy way out. Craig struggled in preschool; he was disruptive and more aggressive than Brian had ever been. At home, he took most of it out on me. I was being verbally and physically abused by my own child. Our quality of life had gone down—way down. And Craig was distraught and unhappy. Just a few months after his diagnosis, we agreed that Craig should start taking methylphenidate. (Craig was, coincidentally, the very age that Brian was when he had begun.) Craig responded to the medication with less hyperactivity and a greater ability to slow down and pay attention.

The next 2 years brought a recurrence of our earlier heartaches. Our visits to doctors (and bills) doubled. I made trips to two schools now to work with teachers on the boys' special needs. Brad, now entering high school, was fed up with his little brothers. Mark and I felt renewed anger and resentment; we had done this once, had "put in our time"—why did we have to do it again? Why us?

Craig's actions now became indicative of Oppositional/Defiant Disorder (ODD). Children with ODD are more blatantly noncompliant than those with ADHD. Children with ODD are *able* to comply with requests but choose not to. Whereas Brian would wander off in the middle of a task, Craig would state, "I'm not gonna do it!" Craig would resist and argue just for the sake of opposing Mark or me. Dr. O— explained the need for clear, consistent rules and firm discipline for children with ODD. Craig's hyperactive behaviors were unintentional and needed to be monitored and guided. But when he was being oppositional, we needed to give him consequences. It was hard, after spending years nurturing Brian, to take a firmer approach with Craig, but I knew that for a good long-term outcome, Craig now needed some "tough love."

Words I had written in this book's first edition came back to haunt me: "Craig's actions began to mirror Brian's." "I feel genuine panic at having to relive those [earlier] days." "I don't know if I would have the stamina to go through this process again." Well, I still don't know if I have it, but we really haven't any choice but to tackle this problem once more. If we don't, the alternatives (and the boys' outcomes) could be worse.

We enrolled Craig in an all-day kindergarten, since he was very bright and liked to be busy. He had a very difficult time following the rules and playing with other children. One classmate spoke loud and clear when she mailed Craig a note that called him the "Master of Madness." Craig made it through only by the constant presence of a guiding adult. His kindergarten was in a parochial school, which is not required to provide support services, so I either went to his school or hired a personal aide to get Craig through the difficult period of lunch and recess.

And once again, the disorder dealt us its backhand blows. Late in kindergarten, Craig developed a hoarse, grating cough that seemed to have no medical basis. When he also exhibited facial tics (such as twitches of his mouth), it became evident that Craig also had Tourette's syndrome (TS). Craig shows other signs of TS: a habit of smelling his fingers after he touches something, aggression (with a dangerous, explosive element), and possibly some speech and language idiosyncrasies. The drug Clonidine decreases Craig's tics and aggression.

We switched Craig to a public school for first grade, which provided services of a speech clinician and a guidance counselor. Craig was several grade levels ahead of most of his classmates in math and reading; his teacher devised ways to appropriately challenge him. She provided Craig with the firm kindness he needed. Most of the time her firmness was enough, but he had episodes that required him to stay after school in detention.

Middle school is bringing a myriad of experiences for Brian. He exhibits a renewal of his earlier intensity, especially in his desire to gain independence from Mark and me. He shuns our attempts to help him, and so much of our guidance is now done "undercover," without his being aware of our efforts. He still lags far behind his peers in the development of many skills, but often just when we think he'll never catch up, he proceeds in leaps and bounds.

Brian's disorder still affects him daily, but it is rare now for him to struggle from morning to night. When he does, Mark and I recall our tried-and-true techniques to help him through.

Over the years we have tried times without Brian's medication, but he simply could not handle himself or his surroundings. Seeing him agitated and "scribbly" again has convinced us that his medication is necessary. By his preteen years, Brian could do pretty well without medication on summer days and some weekends, though he still needed its aid for team activities and for school. He no longer disrupts his class, but on days when he forgets his medication, the teachers say he roams around inattentively or we see an increase in forgetfulness and agitation.

Craig continues on a carefully monitored medication plan: methylphenidate for the hyperactivity and Clonidine for TS.

Brian's hyperactivity has greatly diminished, though early mornings are still difficult for him. Mornings are more than difficult for Mark and me! Craig is boisterous and noisy; Brian is distractible and easily annoyed. They seem to feed off one another's weaknesses.

As with most adolescents with ADHD, Brian's impulsivity has increased; it almost seems a reversion to earlier days. Yet Brian is usually compliant and follows through with things with far fewer prompts and reminders than before.

As Brian matures, he sometimes resents our attempts to guide him. Dealing with homework and trying to organize his time for study, chores, and leisure have created a new source of tension. Mark and I have to be careful not to be overprotective or conspicuous in our guidance. We walk the fine line between guiding him and coddling him, between discipline and punishment, between structure and restriction.

Every developing child must learn to make his own decisions and take responsibility for his actions. Brian and Craig must be held just as responsible as anyone else. In theory I agree with that approach. But given all their struggles, it is hard for me to put into practice. We rightly use the disorder to explain their motives and actions; we try to avoid the danger of using ADHD as an excuse.

In coming years Mark and I will be by our sons' sides less and less. It is crucial that we continue to teach them to do well on their own. Brian will need to make conscious decisions on how to manage his time and talents. As an adult we hope he will direct his energies toward a career that uses his quick mind and attention to detail and downplays his weaker areas like organization.

Craig will likely always struggle with extremes of emotion; his energy, if continued to be properly directed, could bring him great accomplishments. But I shudder to think of the possible outcomes if his intensity and energy become channeled into nonproductive pursuits. I pray that the presence of TS will not seriously complicate Craig's progress.

Brian is well aware of the effect his disorder has had on his life. But little by little he is becoming his own person and making progress. Craig, too, has many more "good" days now than he did even a year ago.

We have already become a closer family because of our struggles. Mark and I are stronger individuals for having worked through our differences, our fears, and our anger. I know I am more compassionate and less judgmental of others than I used to be. Our efforts to understand and deal with our sons' ADHD have been mostly successful and will continue to reap benefits. The disorder will be part of our lives forever, but it does not have to always be a conflictual element. We strive to overcome this disorder and its effects, to look toward a future that our boys can be successful in.

In one study a group of children with ADHD was followed for 20 years; the resulting book, *Hyperactive Chil-*

dren Grown Up, reported that young adults with ADHD tend to be more pessimistic and less confident than their peers (Weiss & Hechtman, 1986). They are generally restless, impatient, and impulsive and exhibit poor social skills.

The *Basic Handbook of Child Psychiatry* (Noshpitz, 1979) stated that the adult with ADHD often lives through "brief friendships, disrupted marriages, inconsistent parenting of his own children, and an unproductive work record." Clinical observations by Drs. Edward Hallowell and John Ratey (1993) agreed, yet also pointed out that adults with ADHD are often "creative, intuitive, [and] highly intelligent" and that "capturing this 'special something' is one of the goals of treatment."

Early diagnosis and treatment are crucial in avoiding such negative outcomes. Our sons were both diagnosed early, and we have done everything we can to provide a supportive environment. We hope they will overcome their obstacles so that their adult lives are minimally affected by their disorder.

Adults with ADHD are bound to struggle to some degree with the residual effects of their disorder. The presence of a supportive spouse, friend, or family member can make their lives easier and more successful. We hope that Brian's and Craig's future will hold loving (and very patient!) people to support them as they continue their personal journeys.

Attention-Deficit/Hyperactivity Disorder can be a burden to live with, yet I firmly believe that every child can be brought to fulfill his highest potential. The attention-deficit part of the disorder can be frustrating for parent and child alike. Yet these children are accepting and very forgiving, even of those of us who so often lose patience with them. Brian is one of these forgiving ones.

The hyperactive part—the child's persistence, energy, and attention to detail—can become great assets throughout life. If we continue to channel Craig properly, he may well do great things with his drive and ambition. Individuals with ADHD have some high hurdles to clear, but they certainly can be successful in careers and personal life.

I often think about children with ADHD who are being raised by uncaring, insensitive parents or parents who refuse to accept the reality of ADHD. My heart aches for these children, and I pray that each will be "discovered" and guided while young enough to be helped. Most parents and teachers are simply unfamiliar with the disorder, as Mark and I were just a few years ago.

For those living with a child with ADHD, the road ahead will be long and often bumpy. I urge those parents to take the initiative to seek out professional help. Even with this help, the parents and child will trip and fall many times along the way. But there is great satisfaction and pride in picking oneself up again. Not all persons will make it as far as they hope. There are many challenges along the way, but our family will continue to travel.

I have some fear letting the boys go into the world this way; for so long I've been their prime protection from what might hurt them. But the fears are lessening. When Craig curbs an angry impulse, when Brian reaches out even a little from his old ways, the satisfaction and joy I feel gives me confidence in their future and makes our family struggles all worthwhile.

References

American Psychiatric Association. (1994). *Diagnostic and statistical manual of mental disorders* (4th ed.). Washington, DC: Author.

Barkley, R. (1992, September). *Proceedings of the regional conference on attention deficit disorders.* Eau Claire, WI: University of Eau Claire.

Barkley, R. (1993, September 24). Paper presented at professional conference, University of Wisconsin, La Crosse, WI.

Department of Behavioral Medicine, Gundersen Clinic. (n.d.). Unpublished handout, La Crosse, WI.

Erickson, M. T. (1983). *Behavior disorders of children and adolescents.* Englewood Cliffs, NJ: Prentice-Hall.

Feeney, S., et al. (1991). *Who am I in the lives of children?* (4th ed.). New York: MacMillan.

Fowler, M., with Barkley, R., Zentall, S., & Reeve, R. (1992). *CH.A.D.D. educator's manual.* Fairfax, VA: CASET Associates.

Friedman, R., & Doyal, G. (1987). *Attention deficit disorder and hyperactivity.* Austin, TX: PRO-ED.

Friedman, R., & Doyal, G. (1992). *Management of children and adolescents with attention disorders* (3rd ed.). Austin, TX: PRO-ED.

Gehret, J. (1991). *Eagle eyes.* Fairport, NY: Verbal Images Press.

Golden, G. S. (1990). Tourette syndrome: Recent advances. *Neurologic Clinics, 8*(3), 705–714.

Goldstein, S. (1993, October). Proceedings of CH.A.D.D. fifth annual conference, San Diego, CA.

Goldstein, S., & Goldstein, M. (1989). *Why won't my child pay attention?* [Videocassette recording]. (Available from Neurology, Learning, & Behavior Center, 230 S. 500 East, Salt Lake City, UT.)

Hallowell, E., & Ratey, J. (1993, Winter). Suggested diagnostic criteria for ADD in adults. *ADDult News.* (Published by Parents of Hyperactive/ADD Children, M. J. Johnson, Ed.)

Hynd, G., et al. (1993). Attention deficit–hyperactivity disorder and asymmetry of the caudate nucleus. *Journal of Child Neurology, 8*(4), 339–347.

Ingersoll, B. (1988). *Your hyperactive child.* New York: Doubleday.

Jordan, D. (1988). *Attention deficit disorder: ADD syndrome.* Austin, TX: PRO-ED.

Jordan, D. (1992). *Attention deficit disorder: ADHD and ADD syndromes* (2nd ed.). Austin, TX: PRO-ED.

LaVoie, R. (1993, October 15). *On the waterbed: The ADD child in the family.* Proceedings of CH.A.D.D. fifth annual conference, San Diego, CA.

Levine, M. (1987). *Developmental variation and learning disorders.* Cambridge, MA: Educators Publishing Service.

Noshpitz, J. (Ed.). (1979). *Basic handbook of child psychiatry* (Vol. 2). New York: Basic Books.

Parker, H. (1988). *Hyperactivity workbook for parents, teachers, and kids.* Plantation, FL: Impact Publications.

Patterson, G. (1976). *Living with children: New methods for parents and teachers* (Rev. ed.). Champaign, IL: Research Press.

Phelan, T. (1990). *1-2-3 Magic! Training your preschoolers and preteens to do what you want.* Glen Ellyn, IL: Child Management.

Schaughency, E., & Rothlind, J. (1991). Assessment and classification of attention deficit hyperactive disorders. *School Psychology Review, 20*(2), 187–202.

U.S. Department of Education, Office of Special Education and Rehabilitative Services. (1991, September 16). *Clarification of policy to address the needs of children with attention deficit disorders within general and/or special education* [Policy Memorandum]. Washington, DC: Author.

Weiss, G., & Hechtman, L. (1986). *Hyperactive children grown up.* New York: Guilford Press.

Zametkin, A., & Hauser, J. (1990). Cerebral glucose metabolism in hyperactivity. *New England Journal of Medicine, 323*(20), 1413–1415.

Zametkin, A. J., & Rapaport, J. (1987). Neurobiology of attention deficit disorder with hyperactivity: Where have we come in 50 years? *Journal of American Academy of Child and Adolescent Psychiatry, 26,* 676–686.

Zentall, S. (1993, October 1). Paper presented at professional conference, Gundersen Clinic, La Crosse, WI.

About the Author

Maureen and her husband Mark live in La Crosse, WI, with their three sons. She is currently a student of psychology, and for the past 4 years has been coordinator of the local CH.A.D.D. organization, a support and education group serving children and adults with attention deficit disorders. Neuville is also a member of the CH.A.D.D. State ADD Council of Wisconsin. She is frequently invited to offer inservice presentations on ADHD to educators and community groups.